CONTENTS

COPYRIGHT AND DISCLAIMER

Disclaimer: the internet is always changing, so the information in this book, although accurate now, may not be 6 months from now. The following articles are simply general tips and helpful advice on assisting you in finding your way around the internet.

ACKNOWLEDGMENTS

I would like to take this space to thank a few people: my wonderful children, Ashley and Jamie who have always been my cheerleaders. They make being a mom a very easy job for me.

My husband, Chris, who doesn't care if I spend too much time working. He understands doing what you love is not work.

And finally my family who think I am a lot smarter than I actually am.

INTRODUCTION

I was recently reminded of the time, when I was driving my daughters and their friends up Springfield Hill to our local park. On our way we saw a man struggling to ride his bike up the hill. With no traffic, I slowed down to cheer him on. The kids joined in. The man smiled and "dug deep" as they say, and actually did make it up that steep hill! Years later, I saw one of the boys that was in the car that day who reminded me of that story. I laughed and said, "Yes, I remember that guy laughing at us but he made it." The boy said, "You were always a cheerleader."

I'm trying to keep that same challenge of encouraging people to not give up – but this time with computers. Believe it or not, computers make our lives much easier. Oh sure they can be frustrating at times because there is so much to be done and sometimes the computer refuses to cooperate. No matter what your user level is, computers can be exasperating.

Hopefully, these articles will give you hope of becoming a computer super-user or at the least comfortable with your keyboard. I have a section of cool tools that will give you some great (mostly free) software and websites that are on the internet to help increase your productivity. Since I speak professionally on the topic, I have a section on social media which will give you some useful tips and information about the different social networks. My true business is building websites so there is a small section on tips for building your own site and information to steer you in the right direction. Internet marketing is such an important factor in having a successful web presence that we need a section for that. And last but not least, your computer and you – a section which will hopefully, help you be comfortable with your computer.

I look forward to cheering you on with your computer and helping you with a variety of tasks and topics. Feel free to email me with any subjects or questions you may have and I'll try to help. Thank you for taking the time to read my book of articles. I really hope you enjoy it and find it useful.

ABOUT THE AUTHOR

Thank you for taking the time to read my book! I'm Tammy Finch, a website designer and social media consultant and the founder of Web Services, Inc. in Peoria, IL. In more than a dozen years in the web design and online marketing industry, I have had the opportunity to work with hundreds of clients, including several in the medical and banking industry, as well as a number of small businesses and associations.

I currently manage more than three hundred websites and social profiles for her clients, and I'm a presenter on the topic of social networking as a business tool. Associations and business audiences around the country have turned to me for workshops on Facebook, Twitter, and LinkedIn, which I feel collectively represent one of the largest untapped opportunities for organizations of all sizes to find new members or customers, improve customer relationships, and even recruit new employees.

Beyond my keynotes and training sessions, I contribute to a number of business publications, both nationally and locally. I'm also available for customized social media consulting and training, and offer social media marketing packages through Web Services, Inc.

You can find out more about me, my presentations, and my services at www.webservicesinc.net.

Section One
COOL TOOLS

HOW TO KEEP YOUR COMPUTER FROM BEING A T.W.

We have all been there, trying to research a question on the internet and find ourselves watching a video of a talking dog. Our computer can certainly be a time-waster or as my husband and I like to say "T.W." It's hard to focus on something with the vastness of the internet. A picture, interesting link or comment catches our eye and before we know it, an hour has passed on a project that was taking 5 minutes. This is a terrible problem for me since I spend a lot of my time on the computer working. I've found a few things that have helped me that I can share.

- Get an egg timer and use it. I found that having a small deadline even if it is sand in a timer, can help use time wisely. Competing against sand to find answers keeps us on track.

- Write it down. Having a checklist on what needs to be done, on and off the computer, really helps keep focus on the work.

- Bookmark your sites. Alt+Z with Internet Explorer and Ctl+D with Firefox will save favorite sites. These will be easily accessible later when there is time to look at the sites. Searching for sites takes time when they aren't easily findable, it is a T.W.!

- Turn off Outlook. Email is always coming through and it will be there when the project is finished. Try not to look at email so often.

◉ Dual monitors. I went kicking and screaming and thought two monitors would take up too much desk space but after a few days of using dual monitors, I will never go back to one. The benefits are wonderful. Two monitors can create a great multitasking environment. All that is needed is a VGA splitter cable and an additional monitor. Set your display to extend and we are off and running!

It's okay to waste time sometimes and a computer is a good source. We have to keep in mind that a computer is also a great learning tool so maybe it's not a waste after all.

COULD A BOOMERANG HELP YOU GET YOUR INBOX UNDER CONTROL?

Buried somewhere in the business and online marketing news in March was the announcement that a popular app – called "Boomerang" – had recently topped one million sales, making the company that developed it a profitable one. While that's certainly something to note for all of those businesses thinking of taking mobile computing to the next level, it's maybe an even more important commentary on the state of our inboxes.

By better allowing users to group, sort, flag, and even re-send the e-mails they get, Boomerang is just the latest in a growing number of tools designed to help you keep in control of your inbox. The fact that such a tool is even necessary is kind of startling in and of itself. But, it's clear that an overflowing inbox has become what stacks of papers piled on a desk used to be: just part of life for a busy working professional.

Luckily, it doesn't take a new app to manage e-mail better. All you need are a handful of tips that will serve you well over time:

Start by setting aside a block of time to sort your e-mail. If, like most of us, you face an inbox each morning that is virtually unmanageable, then "purging" it may be the most important step you can take. It's not going to be fun or pleasant, but setting aside a few hours (with some 15 min. breaks built in) is probably the most effective way to start.

Make a logical set of folders. Most of us don't save our e-mails the way we should because we don't have logical places to put them. Before you begin weeding messages out, make a system of folders to keep the ones you need. These might be sorted by year, client, project, etc., or by some other criteria. All that matters is that it makes sense to you, and you can find what you are looking for later.

Get to know your e-mail program. Along the same lines, most e-mail programs allow you to mark messages with keywords, tag them for later follow-up, and otherwise give them color-coded markings and descriptions. Spending half an hour getting to know your e-mail program now could save you hours and hours of time later.

Observe the five second rule. Productivity experts advise you to spend 5 seconds or less deciding where to put a piece of paper that comes across your desk. Why not do the same with your inbox? If you can quickly determine whether you need to respond, mark it for later follow-up, store it, or delete it, then you have a quick method for getting it out of the way, and out of your mind.

Don't handle e-mail 15 seconds at a time. Speaking of saving time, why deal with every e-mail that comes in right away? Are they all that urgent? Of course not. If you mark off certain times of the day to check e-mail – twice a day is ideal, but even once an hour is an improvement for most of us – you'll stop them from distracting you at other times. Better yet, some problems will have resolved themselves by the time you get around to checking them.

Create a dependable system for follow-ups. Of course, for any of this to work, you have to have a dependable system for following up on issues that need your attention later. Post-its, to do lists, and other traditional time-management tips work well. Just be sure you aren't losing track of issues that are important.

Getting too many e-mails can be a big problem, but you don't necessarily need another app or complicated tool to deal with them. Simply follow these tips, and you'll spend less time sorting through messages each day.

COMPUTERS ARE ACTUALLY EDUCATIONAL TOOLS?

With all the hype of Angry Birds, Facebook's Words with Friends, and other unwanted games on your computer, it is sometimes hard to imagine that we can actually get an education using our computers. Many people are familiar with membership sites such as Lynda.com and Adobe.com. Then of course, the Universities providing online educations, such as Illinois Central College classes or online degrees from the University of Phoenix, but these can tend to be expensive.

To get a degree you must still go to a University but if you just wanted to take a class or learn a new language there are other options available. How about a free education online? It's true. Many websites are providing lectures and course materials free of charge to anyone who would like to sharpen their skills.

Textbook Revolution (http://www.textbookrevolution.org) is a free website run by students who provide a catalog of free textbooks and materials, at no cost. It is a very basic website with a fantastic search function. Everything from Access 2003 to World History can be found here.

Coursera (https://www.coursera.org/) has a seemingly endless supply of classes one could take online. I signed up for the Introduction to Sociology at Princeton University. Before joining the classes, you are provided with information about the class, instructor and the class format. Most of the time, these classes are given by a professor at a large university. What a great way to get familiar with a topic or take a refresher course.

The two websites above were loaded with information and coursework. Most computers can handle the technology needed to "attend" these classes. Basically a pc and a set of computer speakers is all you need. Most of the technology, such as video streams and Blackboards are given on the education website's side. You may need a "plug-in" to view some of the options or coursework, but they are provided by the website for free and are safe to install.

If you don't have time to sit in front of your computer to get smarter, iTunes (itunes.com) has a variety of podcasts that you can download and listen at your convenience. I love listening to them in the car during road trips. My friend, on the other hand, listens to podcasts while she exercises on the walking trails.

However you decide to learn, exercise your brain with these free options.

LET THE NEWS COME TO YOU WITH GOOGLE ALERTS

Do you remember the days when you had to stay up late watching the news on TV to find out how a football game or election turned out? Or do you recall peeking through the back pages of a newspaper searching for a stock price or other piece of non-headline business news?

Most of us who have already had their 30th birthday can recall things like these, and a lot of other instances where the information we were looking for wasn't right at our fingertips. The Internet has changed all of that, of course, by giving us an endless stream of news, information, and even social updates.

But are you getting all of this information as quickly as you could be... and using it to its full potential? Most of us aren't, but Google Alerts can help.

In a nutshell, Google Alerts works like this: You enter in a handful of search terms, topics, or phrases, and Google delivers a report to you when new pieces of news, commentary, video, or other types of content are available. You can easily set the frequency you want to get your updates, so you have the option of receiving updates by the hour, just once a month, or practically anywhere in between. It's like having the world's largest search engine work as your own personal researcher.

How could Google Alerts help you to be smarter and more informed? Here are a few of the most obvious examples:

By delivering you news about your industry, customers, or competitors. No matter what business you're in, it pays to have the right kinds of information at your fingertips. With Google Alerts, you can stay on top of any major developments as they happen.

By helping you to monitor your company's reputation. What are customers, industry observers, and former employees saying about you over the Internet? Google Alerts gives you the option of "keeping an ear to the ground" without having to spend much time or effort.

By giving you an advantage on school or research projects. Whether you're writing a report for the classroom or the board room, it pays to have the most up-to-date information possible. With Google Alerts, you can always be sure that your work reflects the most current information.

By helping you to keep tabs on your favorite things. Recipes, television shows, sports teams, and music groups are just a few of the more obvious examples of interests that you might better stay on top of with Google Alerts.

In reality, there really isn't any limit to what you could better accomplish or manage with a service like Google Alerts. That's because, even though the Internet is constantly placing information at our fingertips, most of us still waste time going out to find it from the same places again and again – requiring us to dig through irrelevant content while possibly missing out on information from better sources.

Here is my advice: Give Google Alerts a try and see what it can do for you. It only takes a few minutes, and it might completely change the way you use the web for years to come.

LIFEHACKER.COM WEBSITE

Do you want to know how to silence your noisy computer -- or how about job hunting advice? Should you trust your head or your gut? These are a few of the items you can find on the website Life Hacker (www.lifehacker.com). Keep your egg timer handy to track your computer time when going to this site or you will be browsing for hours looking at the DIY (do it yourself) section on topics like how to make a built in spice rack.

Content and article websites like these are tough to maintain but Life Hacker has a great supply of information on various topics. It seems that the site is updated several times a day and there is also a Google gadget to plug into your home page.

I highly recommend bookmarking this website for your next "how do I..." question or just for fun and learning.

A FEW BONUS LINKS

Download.com http://download.com/

This website will provide free and safe software for many of your day-to-day activities including LogMeIn, a free software program that you can install on your computer which will allow you to login to your computer from anywhere. This is very handy for travelers or road warriors.

Mashable http://mashable.com/

If you want to find out what's happening on the Internet, this site is for you! There is much more information than you need, but it's easy to pick through.

YouTube http://youtube.com

Do you want to know how to install laminate flooring or how about the best way to cook fish on the grill? This site is will show you a how-to video on just about any topic. It's a great resource of just a fun time waster for watching talking dog videos. I recommend the Ultimate Dog Tease video. Just search for it in the handy search option on the site.

THE MOST USEFUL SOFTWARE AROUND AND ITS FREE

Back in the 90's when I caught the computer bug, I spent way too much time looking for free software programs. I got everything from coloring books for the kids to Tiny Elvis, a small program that would run on the bottom tool bar. Elvis would sit there and watch you work. Then Elvis would randomly stand, and say "Hey man, look at the size of that icon! That sucker is huge!" He would do his dance and sit back down. Classic!

Software has come a long way since Tiny Elvis. Productivity depends on it. Businesses, people, phones, and of course, computers wouldn't be able to work without it. Can we say our lives depend on these programs? Yes, hospitals rely on many types of software for the assortment of machines functioning at their facilities.

Free versions of software are a fantastic way to try out a program before deciding if we want to purchase it or not. My absolute favorite software is Wisdom-Soft Screenhunter. I've used this program for a number of years and feel it is a tool that makes my life much easier. Screenhunter allows the user to capture an image or text on a screen and save it as an image file. All cropping and resizing is done as you capture the file. Simply hit the F6 key to activate the screen hunt, hold the mouse button as you capture the section of the screen you want to capture.

Try it free forever. You can download it today at their website.

http://wisdom-soft.com/products/screenhunter_free.htm

SPENDING HOLIDAY TIME WITH YOUR COMPUTER

I know no one wants to think about the holidays yet, but like it or not, they are coming. We need to get those holiday cards and newsletters out on time. Why not make it easy on ourselves and get a few shortcuts from websites? I don't mean putting a status update on your Facebook page saying "Happy Holidays, everyone!" I mean the real heartfelt holiday cards we get in the mail.

I thought I would share some of my favorite tools to help you make your holiday cards a little brighter.

Microsoft Office Templates
http://office.microsoft.com/en-us/

This website has FREE Microsoft Office templates that you can download to your computer and use for your holiday newsletter, mailing labels or clip art to make your letters more festive. Or get some card stock paper and print your own holiday cards with your ink jet printer.

Avery DesignPro Software
http://avery-designpro.en.softonic.com/

If you have ever worked in an office, you are familiar with Avery Labels. But Avery also has ready to print postcards, badges, brochures or anything else that may be helpful for your office. With that, comes software to print on these products. With over 500 templates with clip art and unique fonts, your holiday correspondence is sure to be the main discussion over dinner.

Find an Address

It's hard to keep track of the family. The larger the family, the more they move around. Anywho.com is a handy tool for looking up a new address: **http://anywho.com**

Go to the website and click White Pages to look up your long-lost relative by name and city. You can even perform a reverse look up if you only have their phone number. The website will give you their contact information if it is listed anywhere on the internet or phone books.

I hope these free online tools will inspire you to start your holiday correspondence. If you absolutely must communication by Email, here are a few links to send personalized electronic cards:

http://www.egreetings.com/

http://www.bluemountain.com/

http://www.123greetings.com/

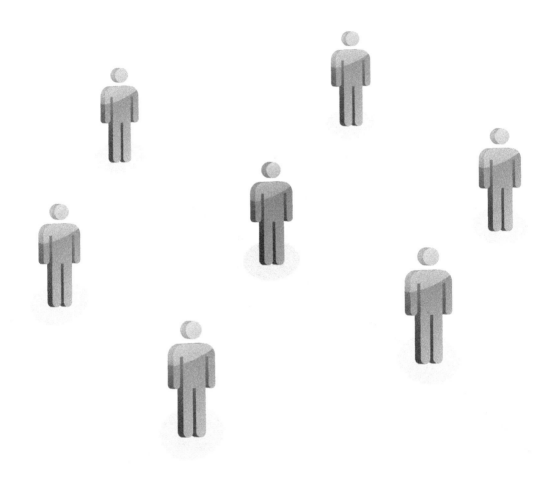

Section Two
SOCIAL MEDIA
MARKETING

SHOULD YOU RESOLVE TO USE SOCIAL MEDIA DIFFERENTLY?

Do you spend more time than you should on social media sites? If you do, you certainly aren't alone: A recent Nielsen study revealed that the average American may spend up to eight hours per month on Facebook alone, with many users logging in a lot more hours.

But for all the handwringing this has brought different companies looking to maximize productivity, and for the amount that we all swear to ourselves that we should "cut back" on social sites a little more, it turns out that the wasted time isn't our biggest concern...

That's because another poll (this one conducted by Harris) says that 63% of respondents say they made social media resolutions for the New Year, but they weren't as concerned about the time they were spending online as they were who it was with. The number one resolution was actually "to share less with fewer people."

While this might seem a bit surprising at first, I think it's more indicative of the changing way that people are thinking about social sites like Facebook, Twitter, and LinkedIn. On the one hand, many of us are recognizing that there's a little too much sharing going on, and that the results can be bad for our reputations, our relationships, and even our chances at staying (or getting) employed in the future.

It may also be a byproduct of information overload. Just as most of us receive far too many e-mails than we can keep up with, our social profiles are crammed with updates, messages, and invitations from others that we just don't have the time to follow up on.

So what should we do with all of this information? Here are four quick ways you should resolve to use social sites differently in the New Year:

Respect privacy. That goes for other people's, of course, but also your own. If you have any doubt about whether or not you should share something online (either because of the way it makes you look, or because a friend, family member or colleague is involved), then it's better to be cautious.

Be friendly in a friendly way. Too many people use social sites the way they would a megaphone, blasting sales pitches, inflammatory opinions, and other obnoxious material without giving it much thought. Treat your friends like friends, not enemies or marketing prospects, and you'll have fewer of them decide to ignore you.

Speak less and listen more. This is a corollary of the same rule, and probably applies well to nearly any area of life. Just as we could all be better listeners off-line, on social media sites it makes us more likable, more genuine, and all-around better people.

Don't let social sites overrun your life. Although it might not be most people's biggest concern, a lot of us probably spend more time than we need to online. Give yourself a regular "diet" of social media time, and then make sure you don't go over your scheduled intake.

In a way, it's strange that social media – something that barely existed five years ago – could be important enough for people to make New Year's resolutions about. It's here to stay, though, so follow their example and get the most out of your profiles in 2012.

IS IT TIME TO DO SOME SPRING CLEANING ON YOUR SOCIAL MEDIA PROFILES?

For most of us, "spring cleaning" involves giving the house a good scrubbing, or maybe putting away those sweaters for another season. But could you stand to do some virtual spring cleaning, too? Specifically, should you look at clearing some space in your social media profiles?

It can make more sense than you might think. We all have contacts that we consistently ignore, or shouldn't have in the first place. It can seem strange to remove those contacts from your social profiles, but sometimes doing that – or at least turning off notifications for their updates – is the smart thing to do. Why? Because most of us spend a lot of our time online in ways that could be better spent elsewhere, or at least better spent on other parts of the Internet. There's just not a good reason to spend a quarter of an hour, or longer, each day digging through posts and updates that aren't important to you.

With that in mind, here are a few guidelines for adding and removing people from your social profiles this spring:

First, remove people you don't like hearing from, those you have a grudge against, or those you broke up with a long time ago. Seriously, who needs the stress? Most of us are busy enough to not have enough time for our loved ones, so stop making time for your unloved ones, especially if you're only holding onto them out of guilt, spite, or some other negative emotion. Those who are more in touch with their spiritual sides might say that letting these kinds of feelings and relationships fester is bad karma; for me, it's just too much of a drag on your schedule and energy level.

Next, add in people you would like to network with, groups you would like to be affiliated with, and those that remind you of your goals. Motivational experts say that you should surround yourself with people who remind you of the person you want to be, and networking gurus will tell you that success is a matter of living and working in the right circles. Either way, what better way to encourage yourself then with daily reminders from the people and organizations who represent your long-term goals? As part of your bigger life plans, make a point of following and networking with others who can help you reach your dreams.

And finally, keep anyone who makes you smile. Regardless of what anyone tells you – on the subject of social networking or anything else – life is short and you should always have a few moments to catch up with an old friend, share a little laugh, or otherwise enjoy a small slice of your day. Social media isn't worth it if you aren't enjoying it, and then again, neither is life.

As spring cleaning season moves into full swing, give some thought to clearing out your social profiles and making them better reflect the person you want to be for the rest of 2012.

3 TRUTHS AND MYTHS IN SOCIAL MEDIA MARKETING

Given that I have been involved with web design and online marketing since the Internet was a "new thing," I've seen a lot of different trends come and go. Some (like usable web design and search engine optimization) become a part of a bigger marketing picture; others fall in and out of favor as they become more or less effective.

One new piece of the puzzle that seems to have a lot of business owners and self-employed professionals intrigued, however, is social media marketing – the art of generating new customers through Facebook, Twitter, LinkedIn, and other social sites. I find that, along with the excitement around social media, there is also a lot of confusion and misinformation.

For that reason, here are three important truths – and myths – surrounding social media marketing:

Truth#1: Social Media Marketing Can be a Powerful Tool For Your Business

The numbers don't lie. In the next year, Facebook and Google+ are both expected to pass the 1 billion-user mark. That means that most of your best customers, colleagues, and networking contacts are all using these sites. What's more, many of them are logging in on a daily basis.

Myth #1: Social Media Marketing is Already More Important than Search Engine Optimization and Other Older Tools

That might be true in certain industries or situations, but most men and women don't go on social sites like Facebook looking to make a purchase. So, while the opportunities are there (especially to have people recommend your company to others), social platforms aren't perfect as marketing mediums just yet.

Truth #2: Social Media Sites Can Help You Build Better Relationships With Customers

There are a lot of reasons that you can use social profiles to build longer-lasting relationships with buyers and increase brand loyalty. For one thing, they allow you to contact customers more frequently and conveniently. Plus, they let you adopt a more personal tone so clients can know you as more than "just another vendor" and even see behind the scenes of your company.

Myth #2: You Should Use Social Media Sites to Turn Customers Into Friends

While it's certainly possible, and not necessarily a terrible thing, for you to reach out to buyers via social sites and turn them into personal acquaintances, that shouldn't be your main goal. Your first objective should be to come across as a competent professional, rather than a potential drinking buddy. One of the biggest mistakes business owners and the self-employed make with social sites is crossing the invisible line of professionalism and hurting their own credibility in the process.

Truth #3: You Can Make Money From Social Media Marketing

Although this should be obvious from the kinds of numbers I pointed to before, there are still people who think that social media marketing is a complete waste of time and money. It isn't. The larger following you have, and the more informed and devoted your customers are, the easier it is to steer them toward your website, online newsletter, and other revenue-generating tools.

Myth #3: Your Social Media Profile is a Great Advertising Platform

You will notice that each of the monetizing strategies above takes buyers away from your social profiles. That's because, as important as they are, they aren't a good place for most businesses to try to ring up sales directly. Use your social profiles to build contacts and credibility; take customers elsewhere (whether it's on the web or not) to finish the transaction.

The bottom line? Social media marketing can be a powerful tool, but only if you approach it the right way, and with the right expectations.

WHAT CAN NORMAL PEOPLE LEARN FROM THE FACEBOOK IPO?

For several weeks now, the arrival of Facebook on to stock exchanges – and into people's investment portfolios – has been in and out of the news. But in some ways this is inevitable: When one of the world's best-known and fastest-growing companies goes public, people are going to take notice. This is a company that's already been the subject of a movie, after all, and it's a story with lots of different characters and billions of dollars floating around.

Assuming, however, that you aren't an investor with millions of dollars to throw at Facebook, or an app mogul trying to spot trends in the digital industry, is all of this just another form of entertainment? Or is there something that normal people can actually learn from the Facebook IPO?

Believe it or not, there are a few lessons for us mortals... and especially those of us who use the Internet as part of our marketing or career growth strategies. Here are a couple of things you can pick up from what's been in the news:

Social media is becoming a big (and I mean big) industry.

The fact that any social media company is being valued in the billions of dollars is an interesting insight. This is a type of company that didn't even really exist just over 10 years ago, and now Facebook is quickly gaining momentum to eclipse the one billion-member mark.

That doesn't just mean it's big business, but also that there isn't really the option to ignore it anymore. Whether you want new customers, better relationships, or future career opportunities, joining up to sites like Facebook, LinkedIn, and Twitter is a good idea.

It's best to diversify your portfolio, and your approach.

While Facebook's entry to the world's publicly traded stocks made big news, it didn't make as much money as expected. These things happen in the investment world, of course, but the realization points to a bigger Internet truth: that you never want to have your eggs all in one basket.

As dominant as companies like Google and Facebook seem today, it's important to remember that their precursors (companies like America Online, Yahoo, and AltaVista) were flying high as recently as a few years ago. While some are carrying on better than others, it makes sense to keep trying new things in your life, your business, and your investment portfolio if you're going to make the most of technology.

Make your online investments carefully.

It doesn't matter if you're looking at stocks, business opportunities, or even memberships to Internet resources. Realize that not everything ends up being the great deal that people think it is, and always do your homework before committing a lot of your time and money to anything new.

One thing I've learned through a lot of years in the web design and online marketing industry is that there is always someone out there ready to help you earn a little more... as long as you don't mind parting with a small fee. Some things end up being great bargains, while others are tough life lessons. More often than not, however, you can spot the great opportunities (and stay away from the wrong ones) by doing your homework and applying some common sense.

That's a good way to do business whether you're investing in a company like Facebook or deciding whether or not to spend a few dollars on that next app – so maybe spending carefully is the biggest lesson of all to take from the Facebook IPO.

HOW SERIOUS IS GOOGLE ABOUT +1?

When you work in the web design and online marketing industry, it can be easy to start seeing Google as that crazy, eccentric genius who works in another building that always seems to be up to something. In a constant effort to redefine the Internet, and the ways we interact with it, they have come up with a host of new ideas: from Google Wave to Gmail and dozens of others.

This is undoubtedly a great thing for most of us, as a whole, but it can also present an interesting challenge: deciding which ones to take seriously and which ones to ignore.

That's because, like any mad genius, Google has been known to get "hot" about a certain topic and then drop it a short time later. If you remembered and understood that reference to Google Wave, then you may already know exactly what I mean – what started out as an ambitious, all-in-one collaboration, communication, and e-mail-replacement product ended up being a cool idea that hasn't gone anywhere just yet. That's not an isolated example, either.

And so, we get to the big question: How serious is Google about +1, its relatively new feature which allows you to "like" different websites, search results, and other content just like you would on Facebook? Is it something you really need to pay attention to... or an interesting thought that probably won't be around in a few months?

There isn't an easy answer to that question, so here are a few ways to think about things:

If you market your business online, you should encourage customers to +1 you.

If +1 catches on, then it seems likely that Google will incorporate the opinions of searchers and customers into its results sometime in the future. In other words, the more people who +1 your site now, the more of them you may be able to attract to your business in the future.

+1 allows you to make the world's largest search engine better.

Lost in all of this is the sort of "civic opportunity" that +1 represents. After all, one of the most frustrating things about using Google – or any search engine – is that it sometimes can't give you the result you're really looking for. By voting for certain sites over others, you might be able to make it easier for people just like you to find the information they want faster.

We'll all know more about +1 soon enough.

Google's push to make +1 a mainstream idea seems destined to either succeed or fail pretty quickly. It's a good bet that we'll know within the next few months whether it's catching on or not, so there probably isn't a rush to get involved.

My best advice? Give +1 a try and see what you think. The web may or may not need a social component to search engine listings, but the mad geniuses at Google have done enough great things before to earn the benefit of the doubt.

SORTING OUT ALL THINGS SEARCH AND SOCIAL

In the same way that successful comedians eventually yearn to become serious actors, and serious actors strive to become rock stars, it seems only inevitable (in retrospect) that Google, Facebook, and Twitter seem to want to be more like each other... or at least they want to do whatever they can to eat up each other's share of online attention and marketing dollars.

You can see this in the way that Google is pushing its +1 feature, and in the recent decision by the executives at Twitter to add more keyword and search features, making tweets and other forms of content easier to find. Facebook, also, has taken a handful of steps (with usernames and profile features) seemingly designed to make the site easier to search.

Clearly, they all strive to be one of the biggest players in both categories, not just one. So, as search engines integrate social features and social sites try to be more search-friendly, it's time to ask: will there ever be an all-in-one website that integrates search and social together?

While it's possible that one or the other will eventually win out and become the overwhelming public favorite for both social use and searching – Google and Facebook would be the best picks here – it probably isn't going to happen soon. And believe it or not, even though that means keeping track of different websites and profiles, that might not be a terrible thing.

Here are three reasons why:

Search and social media have separate uses.

Typically, users who log on to social sites are looking to meet up with friends, make a personal connection, or maybe just share a few thoughts or photos. Search engines, on the other hand, are typically portals to information as well as products and services. That means that any site that does extraordinarily well with search, for example, probably won't fare quite as well as a social medium, and vice versa.

Social media has limited business value, for now.

Don't get me wrong: I spend a good deal of my time teaching businesses all the reasons that social media is one of the most powerful marketing tools they can use. So it's not that the business value isn't there, just that it's on more of a one-on-one personal level. The kinds of things businesses use search engines for, on the other hand, have more of a mass-marketing feel. There's nothing wrong with either!

The competition is good for everyone.

In the end, even though Google, Yahoo, and Twitter may secretly hope to put each other out of business, it's in our best interests if they don't. After all, the harder they work to battle each other, the more creativity and innovations come to the rest of us – often completely for free.

With that in mind, there's really no rush to find a "winner" in the battle between search and social media, because there may never be one, and we probably wouldn't wish for it anyway.

THE POWER AND MYSTERY OF TWITTER

A few years ago I didn't get it either. How could the babble on Twitter make a difference in marketing a business and engaging customers? I tried several times to come up with some witty, keyword rich Tweets that would get the attention I wanted, but I didn't have much luck.

The other day, I read another article about a customer who tweeted a receipt from a pizza place with a racial slur on it. It wasn't a complaint directly to the company. She only tweeted a picture of it to her friends. However, it was re-tweeted (shared or forwarded) until 200,000 people viewed it within 24 hours, including the media. Now, she is bombarded with requests for interviews, the pizza place is scrambling to fix the situation and she is laying low until everything "blows over".

There seems to be no sense to this social network. But I do like how it works. Sysomos.com, a subsidiary of Marketwire Inc., says 92% of retweets happen in the first hour. Therefore, it's not easy to actually delete a message here. Tweets get re-tweeted in an instant. Ask some of the celebrities who have Tweeted in the heat of the moment and back-pedaled trying to fix what they said.

Twitter is fun! I love watching the Academy Awards and following the Tweets at the same time. It is like watching the show with a million others. People are so witty and some of the comments were hilarious. Twitter is informative if we view it as a news feed. And believe it or not – it's valuable. I've changed my view of the social network and lightened up. Sometimes, I still don't get it but can see it works well. I think being active with social networks and leveraging yourself against the competition is what is going to work for business. If not, I'll still enjoy the Tweets of others.

I would love to hear any success stories with Twitter from others.

EIGHT RULES FOR TWITTER SUCCESS

Twitter isn't just the newest of the major social media sites, but also the one that's growing (and changing) the fastest. Given that tweeting was mainly reserved for certain types of athletes, celebrities, and Internet addicts only a few years ago, it's pretty amazing to sit back and see what it's become.

That "it" that Twitter has become poses an interesting challenge to marketers, though. On the one hand, your Twitter profile is a great way to reach large groups of people at once; and the other, it takes something special to stand out in the virtual crowd and get significant numbers of followers in the first place.

So, how do the very best do it? That's easy – they just follow the eight Golden rules of Twitter marketing:

1. Don't be "just another tweeter."

From custom-designed profile skins to catchy usernames and a unique writing voice, it's important for users to be able to tell you apart from all the others in your industry.

2. Be honest and credible on Twitter.

The world doesn't need more loud, uninformed, or disingenuous voices, on Twitter or elsewhere. But, if you can give people honest and helpful insight, you'll develop a reputation for being someone worth reading.

3. Tweet for a large audience.

Your goal when you tweet shouldn't just be to inspire ideas or actions amongst your followers. If you can write something interesting enough for them to re-tweet to others, your efforts are instantly multiplied.

4. Share anything that's useful.

While you don't want to plagiarize tweets ideas from other people, there isn't anything wrong with passing along links, thoughts, ideas, and facts that you've picked up elsewhere. As long as you're a source of useful information, people won't worry about where it came from (just be sure to reference the original source).

5. Think beyond text.

Some of the best tweets don't even involve 140 characters. Not only can you post something that's even shorter, but you can also include things like pictures, or even links to YouTube videos.

6. Know your hashtags.

Using the right hashtags on your tweets can help make your messages easier to find, or put them in their context as part of a bigger trending thought or idea. Look at the way some well-known marketers or celebrities use theirs, and you'll get a good sense of how to place hashtags in your own tweets.

7. Be careful about what you share.

One of the things that has made Twitter so well-known in such a short amount of time is the propensity that celebrities have for sharing thoughts (and sometimes body parts) that would have been better kept to themselves. Learn from their blunders, and don't share anything you wouldn't want certain employees, competitors, or potential customers to see.

8. Don't rely on Twitter alone.

You're unlikely to make much money directly from your tweets, but what you can do is use a strong Twitter following as a source of traffic for your blog, or to direct people to articles or pages on your website.

With Twitter, it's never been easier to create a marketing impact with 140 characters at a time. Make sure you follow these rules and tweet with your goals in mind, though, or you'll have a hard time standing out in the crowd.

WHAT IS BEING SAID ABOUT YOU ON LINKEDIN WHEN YOU AREN'T THERE

Of all the social networking sites out there, LinkedIn is the one that attracts the most attention from business-minded men and women. After all, it's the only major social site that's completely devoted to making professional connections. For that reason, you're a lot more likely to find CEOs and other VIP contacts on LinkedIn than you are on any other Internet destination.

But, while LinkedIn might draw the most interest, it also tends to be the least "social" of the major networking sites, since users tend not to post as often or share as many personal details.

That can lead business owners, self-employed professionals, and other marketers to set up basic LinkedIn profiles and then forget about them. That can actually almost be worse than having none at all, since LinkedIn profiles tend to rank very highly on Google and the other major search engines. So, when potential customers, employees, and vendors go looking for information about you or your business, they are very likely to come across your LinkedIn profile before finding anything else.

For that reason, it's important that your LinkedIn profile is doing its job as a social media marketing tool. It needs to be one of your strongest Internet advocates, not simply a description with your name and current position.

Here are a few quick tips for getting more from your LinkedIn profile:

1. Fill out your entire profile.

As I've already mentioned, lots of people like to fill in basic info and leave it at that. Even though it can be time-consuming and tedious, you need to go further and be sure that things like your photo, job history, and special skills or certifications are mentioned. The time you spend will be well worth the effort when new customers view your profile and come away impressed.

2. Get lots of customer recommendations.

Just as important as the information you fill in about yourself – or maybe even a lot more important – is what other people say about you and your work. The more recommendations you have from former customers, clients, employees, or colleagues, the easier it is for people to feel comfortable deciding to do business with you.

3. Join groups and participate in discussions.

This is perhaps the biggest missed opportunity on LinkedIn. Don't let your profile simply be static. Instead, network with others, start discussions, and participate in all the growing communities around your industry. The connections you make with colleagues and prospects could end up being priceless.

4. Keep things current.

The last thing you want is to build a powerful LinkedIn profile that lots of people can find easily, only to have it get out of date. It's particularly important that things like your contact information and current job position are accurately reflected, as you definitely want someone who's interested in contacting you for an exciting opportunity to be able to do so.

LinkedIn can be a wonderful aid in promoting your own business or career. Just make sure you give it enough time and attention. Before long, it could be just what you need to introduce yourself to a whole new group of executives and high-profile customers!

DISCOVER THE POWER OF SOCIAL NETWORKS FOR FINDING A JOB

Finding a job can be a frustrating process. There are many ways you can find a job offline and online. However, one of the fastest growing methods is networking through social network sites. Social network sites can be an extremely valuable tool that will help you learn of job opportunities that are not even posted.

While social network sites have become the more popular way to find a job, it can be overwhelming because of the increase of social network sites created. It is important to know what you are doing when promoting yourself on one of these sites, or you can leave the wrong impression. This article will give you some ideas on what you need to do to succeed in finding a job through social networks.

Benefits of Using Social Networks

◉ Establishes a professional online presence that will present your skills and accomplishments.

◉ Allows you to find others interested in your field of work and connect with these people for advice and knowledge they have in this area.

◉ Helps you to identify employers and key contacts within a company you are targeting. This will increase your invisibility as a candidate.

- Allows you to create a well designed profile for recruiters to view.

- Allows you to create relevant information and supply resources relevant to your industry.

- Helps you to generate referrals.

Tips for Using Social Networking to Find a Job

While social networking is one of the best ways to search for a job, it can completely damage your credibility and/or chances of being hired if you are not careful in your approach. There are many mistakes you can make during your social networking campaign for finding a job. If you follow these tips, you may be able to avoid these mistakes and have a successful outcome.

Complete your Profile

Your profile is basically your resume. You will want to make sure you complete the profile extensively. If your profile is not complete, this could deter a person from connecting with you because there is not enough information up front for them to make an informed decision. Go through each step and include any and all information you can about your experiences and employment history.

Research yourself

This is important because this is exactly what an employer who is interested will do. See what is out there when you type in your name. Make sure you are aware of anything that is negative associated with your name. This way you will be prepared to defend yourself, rather than be shocked at what is being reported. More than likely, the negative information is not even regarding you, but someone with your same name. However, this way you will be prepared to explain this information. To do this, simply do a Google search.

Remember Proper Etiquette

Just because you are online does not mean you should throw proper etiquette out the door. Being online might give you that little bit of extra confidence you need to approach a person that you would not normally have face to face; however, it is important that you are not too forward in your approach. Don't forget the "small talk." This will help you build a rapport with that person where you can then transition into talking about the employment opportunity.

Utilize Social Networking Tools and Apps

Enhance your online image by using the tools they provide. These tools can truly add depth to your profile, which can enhance your professional image.

Top Social Networks for Finding a Job

- LinkedIn

- Facebook

- Plaxo with Simply Hired

- Twitter with Blog or LinkedIn URL

You may need to combine some methods to help you increase your chances for employment. For example, you are more likely to find a job through Twitter if you connect it with a blog or LinkedIn URL.

Social networking is an excellent resource for searching for that dream job. Just remember that your approach can truly impact your chances of finding that perfect job. A professional image is extremely important. Take care to protect your online image, and you could be on your way to a lucrative career.

4 WAYS JOB SEEKERS CAN USE THE INTERNET TO BUILD A BETTER CAREER

If this economy has thrown you back into the job market – or if you have decided that it's the right time to make a career move – then you probably already know that the Internet could be your top resource for finding a new job. Even if you have a big network of personal contacts and the kind of resume that would put most CEOs to shame, the chances are good that you could at least make things quicker and more efficient by putting the power of the web on your side.

That's common knowledge, but I regularly meet people who aren't exactly sure how that process should work. They want to use the Internet to help build a better career, but aren't sure how.

Because finding a new job can be a difficult and frustrating process already, I'd like to offer some quick and easy tips candidates can use to get hired. Here are my five favorite:

1. Build (and clean up) your social media profiles.

In many ways, finding a job is still about who you know. You don't necessarily have to have connections in the company or industry you want to work for, but having recommendations, common professional acquaintances, and association contacts is a strong starting point. Just make sure you don't have a post, information, or photos that will embarrass you or give someone second thoughts about interviewing you.

2. Create an online resume or personal website.

You could simply upload your resume to sites like Monster and Career Builder, but why not go a step farther and create a website with your resume, photos, recommendations from friends and colleagues, and maybe even an online "virtual interview" video? The technology for all of these tools makes them relatively inexpensive, and you can bet they'll separate you from the hundreds of other candidates who can only show a piece of paper.

3. Scour the job boards.

Once you have your supporting materials in place, it's worth noting that you shouldn't ignore sites like Monster and Career Builder (not to mention Craigslist and industry sites). Employers in human resources departments like them, so they can be valuable resources. Just know that there is an art and science to getting noticed in these kinds of digital settings, so make sure your resume has the right kinds of keywords and phrases, because it may have to pass a digital software check long before an actual human will see and review it.

4. Take online courses and earn certifications.

Sometimes, the best way to move yourself into a new career isn't to get in touch with more employers, but to make yourself more employable. It's easier than ever to find and take courses online (from simple weekend certifications to college-level classes), and they could make the difference between being interviewed and staying at home. Continual learning is a must in almost any job because it doesn't just keep you "up with the times," but also shows that you have the ambition to stay on top of your field.

Could you be using the Internet to get more from your job search (or just get hired faster)? I hope these tips will help you get moving in the right direction. Give them a try and be sure to let me know when they work for you!

As a stock, there may be a lot of questions surrounding Facebook's value. But as a social media marketing tool for business owners, executives, and self-employed professionals, its power is easy to understand. With more than 500 million users already registered – and a good percentage of them coming to the site on a daily basis – it represents one of the most popular destinations on the Internet.

> *In other words, you need to be on Facebook as a marketer because so many of your customers (both current and potential) already are.*

But, making Facebook part of your Internet marketing plan takes more than a simple profile and a handful of invitations for your closest friends and colleagues. Here are some easy-to-follow steps you can take to get more from Facebook marketing immediately:

1. Fill your profile with the right content.

Your business profile (or fan page) should be a marketing tool first and foremost. For that reason, it's important you add things like your phone number and company website, along with businesslike pictures and descriptions. That's especially true for self-employed professionals, who can sometimes fall into the trap of mixing in too much personal information. If necessary, create different profiles for yourself and your company.

2. Start with who you know.

Although I've already mentioned that you shouldn't be satisfied with simply adding your existing friends and colleagues to your Facebook network, they do make an excellent starting point. The more friends and fans you have in the beginning, the easier it is for other people to find out about you and make their own connections.

3. Give people a reason to connect with you.

Speaking of making connections, don't assume that potential customers are going to do it simply because they want to know you. Instead, offer things like discounts, specials, or even product and industry advice via your Facebook fan page. These will give new contacts a reason to connect with you, not to mention spread the word to their friends.

4. Begin conversations, not sales pitches.

Remember that social media is all about two-way conversations, not flat-out marketing messages. It's important that your updates not read like a pay-per-click ad. Instead, they should be short, insightful comments or articles that invite customers or colleagues to follow up and engage you. Outside of online marketing, we call this "building relationships," and it's the foundation of social media success.

5. Use contests, external links, and other tools to jumpstart sales.

Eventually, you'll want to find a way to turn your growing network into something that helps you make more money. There are a lot of ways to do this, but the easiest is to give your friends and fans a good reason to leave your Facebook profile and visit your business website. Contests and other promotions can be the perfect nudge to help them discover things like online videos, landing pages, and product descriptions.

Facebook can actually become a valuable part of your marketing mix if you're willing to treat it as more than just a place to post vacation photos and complain about your day. Follow these quick tips, and you'll be turning friends into fans – and fans into customers – in no time at all.

SOCIAL MEDIA IS GETTING EVEN EASIER

For all the wonderful things social media can do for your business, a lot of our clients do have one tiny complaint: they just don't have enough time to update their own profiles and content, much less pay attention to what's going on in the social networking universe.

That's not a very good excuse for failing to get the most out of Facebook, Twitter, and LinkedIn. After all, few of the other activities you're going to do in a workday could potentially open you up to tens of millions of new customers, and using social networking sites tends to be as much fun as it is work. Still, for those of you who are hanging on to a lack of time as your reason for not getting involved, we're going to fill you in on something important – it's getting even easier to stay on top of your social media marketing...

All you need are the right tools.

There are lots of new websites and applications out there that can help you manage your social profiles, search new content, and even keep track of all kinds of analytics. If you are new to social media tools, however, there are two in particular you should definitely check out:

HootSuite (http://hootsuite.com) is a social media hub, allowing you to create a dashboard from which you can monitor all your social accounts from one place. Whether you're on a desktop, or connecting to the

Internet via a smart phone, it's a great way to keep an eye on your stats, customers, and everything else from one convenient location.

TweetDeck (http://www.tweetdeck.com) is a similar service with a slightly different layout and feature set. It has better Facebook and LinkedIn integration, and also allows you to add video to your profiles more easily, but doesn't offer quite as much in the way of metrics and reporting.

Which one is right for you and your business?

That's tough to say. Since they both do the same kinds of things, but in a slightly different way, why not try them both and see which one is a better fit? Regardless of whether you prefer HootSuite, TweetDeck, or one of their lesser-known competitor's, one thing will be clear: you just ran out of excuses not to make the most of social media marketing.

CAN PINTEREST BE GOOD FOR BUSINESS

As a business owner, by now you've probably realized the power of social media. Social media sites like Facebook, Twitter, and Google have moved to the forefront when it comes to social interaction on the web. But surely other companies continue to innovate, and bring new ideas forward?

Enter Pinterest.

Pinterest is a sharing community, where users can create and manage image collections based on topics or themes. New pieces are "pinned" to a given board, and other users can comment or re-pin them to their own.

Sounds good, but how can Pinterest help your business?

Since Pinterest is primarily visual, it allows you as a business owner to easily create and share themed content with your customer base. They, in turn, can re-pin what you post and increase the spread of your business name and profile. Be it a selection of photos from a recent promotional event, a series of exercises for health and fitness, or a delicious recipes that use your products, your pins have the potential to go viral in the same way as posts on other social networks!

So check out Pinterest today, and explore new ways of integrating it into your social media campaigns.

5 WAYS THE SPA INDUSTRY CAN MAKE THE MOST OF PINTEREST

Is your company using Pinterest as an online marketing tool? It's one of the fastest-growing social media sites out there, and there is still plenty of room for growth.

If you aren't familiar with the site yet, the basic idea is that it's a social media hub that's built around images and lists. In other words, users post pictures and then start discussions around them, with the normal give-and-take that's common on other sites like Facebook and Twitter. Because things are image-based, and because Pinterest has a unique following, it offers some marketing opportunities that other companies can't match. In my opinion, the spa industry can really take advantage of this site with some attractive images.

If you haven't stopped by the site yet, set up your free account and look around. Then keep in mind these five things businesses of all sizes can do to make the most of Pinterest:

1. Gather more social media recommendations.

Like any social site, Pinterest gives you a chance to have your customers spread the word about your products for you. And because they're using images, the effect can be that much more powerful. To see what we mean, just take a look at some of the "pinboards" that have already been started – you'll see immediately how easy it would be for the right discussion to boost interest in your products.

2. Get people talking.

There are probably dozens, or hundreds, of ideas you have for topics about your exclusive products or the spa industry. Why not start one, post some images, and see where it goes? At best, you'll get lots of valuable insight and some great referrals. At worst, you'll have tried something new inbuilt a few more links back to your company's website.

3. Market more effectively to women.

Although this may change over time, the early evidence suggests that Pinterest is especially popular with women. That means that, if your spa is targeted to them, then Pinterest could represent a more efficient way to reach them. That's especially true when you consider how crowded Facebook and Twitter have become recently.

4. Take advantage of great photos.

Great photos make a big bottom-line difference on your website, but why not get even more mileage out of them by using them to start pinboards on Pinterest? The right picture truly can be worth a thousand words, or more, so having yours on more social sites can only be a good thing from a marketing perspective.

5. Get better feedback from customers.

As with all social media sites, the biggest benefit from using Pinterest might not be in the opportunities to market to new customers, but to get feedback from the ones you already have. Because social networking allows for a one-on-one communication that's hard to duplicate over the Internet, your buyers might tell you things you couldn't learn otherwise, but only if you sign up and start a new discussion.

MANTERESTING STUFF!

Well, it was bound to happen with the Pinterest.com craze – Pinterest type sites for men. For those of you who aren't familiar with Pinterest, it's a social network that is focused on pictures. Users "pin" pictures to their boards and people like, comment or share. Like many social networks, they get their start with a certain industry. For example, lots of graphic designers, foodies and artists were joining Pinterest before it caught on to everyone else. At a recent workshop for a spa convention, I recommended they all join Pinterest. The spa industry is very visual and that seems to be what Pinterest is all about. Recently, I saw a few construction companies posting before and after pictures of their work on Pinterest. What a great idea!

But now, how about a website that isn't so, well girly? How about something that is focused on men and their muscle cars, man caves and zombies. I give you MANteresting.com! Going to this website reminds me of reading a Hot Rod magazine or watching The Man Show on television. Not really something for me, but if you are a guy, take a look at what MANteresting.com has to offer. It's easy to use like Pinterest but more focused on men and their interests. In fact, I found a couple more of these types of sites:

http://dudepins.com

http://www.dartitup.com

SOCIAL MEDIA FOR THE MEDICAL INDUSTRY: HOW MUCH INFO IS TOO MUCH?

Privacy on the Internet is always been a bit of a dicey topic, and the lines between what is acceptable and what isn't are still a bit blurry. In recent weeks, major companies like Apple, Sony, and Google have gotten into trouble with consumers and governmental agencies alike for the way they collect and distribute information about their users... and there's no sign that these struggles are going to let up any time soon.

Add in the stiff regulations and penalties that medical groups are already facing in regard to patient information, and it's easy to see why so many of them are reluctant to touch social media at all – whether it's through sites like Facebook, Twitter, and LinkedIn, or through their own company blogs and newsletters.

Still, there are compelling reasons for hospitals, healthcare practices, elder care facilities, and other medical industry organizations to get involved with social media and reap the benefits that other businesses are. Here's what you need to know to get started and stay out of trouble:

Social media can be a big boost to your organization.

For one thing, hundreds of millions of people are flocking to social media sites, which should be reason enough for you to test the waters. More than that, your company's blog and other content can be a great way to share information, invite feedback, and attract interest from potential customers or patients at the same time.

Few things are truly private on the Internet.

The key to making your social media strategy safe is setting strong guidelines for all employees at the beginning of the process – not after you have complaints or problems. Make sure everyone on your team knows what is and isn't appropriate to share, and then review everything before it goes public... because that's what your social updates really are.

Start discussions, but avoid specifics.

There are lots of ways to tell people about your facilities and services without mentioning specific patients or sharing photos of the men and women in your care. Get in the habit of sharing broad information and introducing important topics. The more you say about the issues people care about, and the less you share about individual situations, the easier time you're going to have navigating social media.

WHY SOCIAL MEDIA AND THE SPA INDUSTRY WERE MADE FOR ONE ANOTHER

These days, there are few businesses that can afford not to be involved in social networking sites like Facebook, Twitter, and LinkedIn. But for the owners and managers of spas and salons, the need to set up profiles and start marketing is particularly critical. That's because the spa industry, like few others, is uniquely positioned to take advantage of the social media boom in terms of short bits of content and a lot of new customers.

Here are three quick reasons that social media sites and the spa industry were practically made for one another:

What's more social than a spa?

People don't just love getting personal treatments, they love telling other people about them, too. The social nature of the activity itself – do most of your customers come alone, or with a close friend or relative? – means that they'll be more open to sharing about themselves, and their experiences.

The success of a spa is all about the customer experience.

Your reputation is everything, and there is no easier way to spread some positive word of mouth for your studio then having satisfied customers post positive reviews on your Facebook fan page, or tweet them to friends. Not only do these activities help you bring in new customers by showing that you do good work, but they help your search engine profile at the same time, too.

New mobile device apps are making it easier for customers to drop in.

Anyone with an iPhone, Droid, or other smart phone can get instant updates that lead them to the nearest spa, inform them about specials, help them make an instant appointment, and so much more. If your customers are on the go, and they very likely are, then taking advantage of social media and mobile web apps could lead to a significant increase in business. Are you taking advantage?

FACEBOOK AND SOCIAL MEDIA NETWORKING – TOP 5 REASONS TO USE IT

Social media is growing rapidly and with that growth, its importance to business is expanding. Once widely considered a youthful fad, social media is now being used for many legitimate business purposes. In the latest 2010 statistics, Facebook, has over 500 million users and 34% use Facebook for their business. 20 million people become "fans" of business pages each day. LinkedIn boasts 80 million users, which represents a growth of 5 million since December 2009. Twitter has grown from approximately 5,000 "tweets" per day in 2007 to a reported 65 million tweets a day as of June 2010. Social media is not just for kids: YouTube recently reported that 57% of its videos are posted by users from 20 to 35 years old -- 20% by users over 35.

These types of statistics clearly indicate social media is not going away. By now, we all know that social media is a cost-effective way of marketing your company and educating clients. But what are some of the other reasons to use Social Media Marketing?

Connection with Customers:

This should be the main reason for using Facebook, LinkedIn, YouTube, or other networking sites. You can easily maintain contact with customers on LinkedIn, as well as quickly build a network of other connections through their contacts. Creating affiliations can be as simple as signifying your "like" of a customer's Facebook page. Listening is the first rule of thumb with good customer service. With social networking sites, you can follow what is happening in your customers' companies so you can be more responsive to their needs.

Search Engine Optimization:

Did you know that messages posted on your Facebook Business page are searchable on Google? By considering how customers will search for you and including those keywords in your posts, you can generate more search results about your company. For instance, if you were to post "ABC Roofing is working in Peoria, IL today replacing shingles on XYZ Company's main building," potential customers searching for "ABC Roofing," "Peoria, IL," or "XYZ Company" in Google would quickly find a link to your post. This increases your visibility and gives clients a better chance of finding your company on the vast Internet.

Keep up with the Joneses:

Most people look online for products and services. In fact, Google boasts 80% of consumers go online to find products and services rather than the telephone book. Your competitors may already be using social media to connect with their customers. Why not use any means available to spread the word about your own company? We've all heard of musicians using YouTube to get discovered, or the Old Spice YouTube/ Twitter campaign, which was very successful. But businesses can benefit from video marketing also. A Utah company, BlendTech, created simple YouTube video demonstrations of their product blending everything from golf balls to cell phones. As a result, their sales increased 700%!

The Price is Right:

Marketing your company through social media costs nothing more than your time. It's very easy to use, which makes it attractive to busy business owners. As with anything else, social media gets easier the more you use it. Using short-cut tools such as www.ping.fm can save even more time online.

Recommendations:

Customer testimonials have long been an effective marketing tool for businesses. We all know that most people will ask for referrals from friends when searching for a professional service. When satisfied customers have the opportunity to post comments about their experience with you on a social media site, their positive reviews instantly reach a large network of contacts. In addition, more people are likely to watch a video or click a link sent by a family member rather than the company itself.

Having that instant connection to your customers and listening to their needs puts you ahead of your competition. Your business referrals coming online are shared easily and economically. From a business standpoint, we can't ignore 500 million users on Facebook. We've seen the effects of social media for our own small business customers at Web Tech Services, Inc. Many of our clients have seen an increase of website traffic by 50%! This reason alone should motivate you to start your new social media campaign. While you may not get a 700% increase in business as BlendTech, you will have your customer's appreciation for being easily accessible on the internet.

WHY SHOULD YOU HIRE A SOCIAL MEDIA CONSULTANT?

Social media marketing – that is, the art and science of finding new customers through sites like Facebook, Twitter, and LinkedIn – is still incredibly new, even by Internet standards. Already, however, there are certain trends that are emerging, and certain advantages that small business owners are excited about. One of the most prominent is that social media runs on creativity and attention, as opposed to big budgets, which means it can effectively provide smaller companies with the chance to reach new markets almost for free.

So why is it, then, that so many web design and online marketing firms (like ours) will advise you to consider hiring a social media consultant? The answer is simpler than you might think: because for anything to be cost effective, it has to be effective first.

That's an important point, because we come across all kinds of small businesses who are eagerly trying to get involved with social network marketing – and are devoting all kinds of time and energy to it – but aren't getting the results they hoped for. Having someone who knows the landscape, and has an outside perspective on your businesses online marketing efforts, can be a big help.

Here are 3 quick ways a social media consultant can help turn your profiles and content into something that can help you win more business:

By making regular updates.

Social network marketing might not take a lot of money, but it still does require an investment of time. That's something a lot of our clients don't have, and so it's no surprise that they can't post as many updates and pieces of new content as they would like. Having a social media consultant who keeps your accounts up to date is a great way to solve this problem.

By keeping you on message.

Social media for businesses that are trying to find customers is different than having a set of personal accounts. That's why it's so important that you stay positive, professional, and on message – three things an outside consultant can do for you.

By helping you find new things to try.

What's working on Facebook and the other major social media sites today might not be tomorrow. But few business owners have time to keep up with all the latest tips and trends. For that reason, having someone who can devote time and energy not only to your accounts, but to the industry as a whole, can make all the difference.

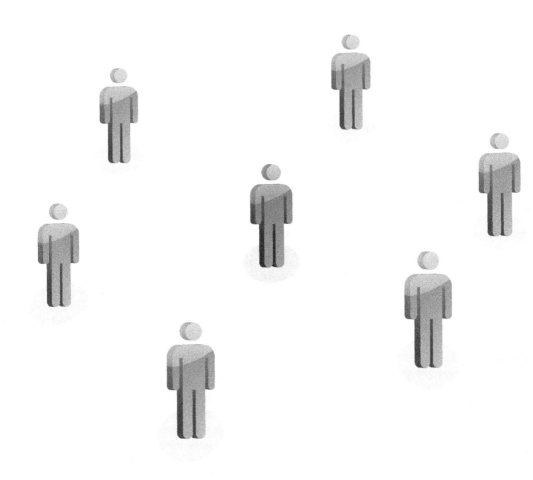

Section Three
WEBSITE STRATEGIES

WHAT MAKES A "NOT SO GREAT" WEBSITE?

Have you ever clicked through a link to a website and found something that made you literally cringe? As an experienced business web designer, I have to say that I have this unfortunate experience a couple of times every week. While websites can be considered art, and subject to a lot of different tastes, there are some that are simply terrible by almost anyone's standards.

It's enough to make you wonder: Why is it that people – and especially businesses – put up awful websites in the first place, much less keep them around? After spending a while on this question, the only answer I can think of is that they simply don't know how bad they are. Like the YouTube clips you sometimes see of tone deaf men and women belting out covers of their favorite tunes, there are a handful of people who really do think they have awesome websites, when in reality they are driving visitors in another direction.

So what exactly makes a terrible website? Although individual opinions may vary, here are some things I think almost all of us can agree upon:

Missing pages and broken links.

While these might not be the first things you think of when it comes to "terrible" websites, it is incredibly frustrating to be looking for a product, answer, or detail only to find that what you are searching for is no longer there – or maybe wasn't in the first place.

If something is supposed to be on the website and isn't, that's going to be a major annoyance for a lot of people who come in as visitors... and they won't stay long.

Overused music and animations.

When was the last time you visited a website that automatically started playing music or animations and thought, "Wow, this is really great!" Don't worry; I really can't remember that happening, either.

What's worst about these types of websites is that they just assume you like the same things that the web designer did. Unfortunately, not everyone has the same tastes, and even if we did, being interrupted by unexpected music and animations when we are surfing the Internet is just plain annoying.

Repetitive writing.

Unless you happen to own a business or work in online marketing, you might not realize that Google and the other major search engines give you results by searching the text within websites and trying to match up relevant results to important terms and phrases. This leads web designers to do some pretty crazy things to get Google to notice, including repeating the same term or phrase over and over and over and over...

Once upon a time, that was a good way to attract people to your website (believe it or not). Now, not only does it not work, but it's a big turn-off for actual humans who have to read the pages.

Marketing that's **OVER THE TOP.**

In the same way, the huge amount of competition between competitors in nearly every business has led some companies to take an infomercial-style approach to writing. No matter what it is you want, they can promise to give it to you faster, cheaper, and better, but only if you ACT NOW!!!

It kind of goes without saying that no one falls for this anymore. In fact, the only thing over-hyped marketing messages are good for is driving customers away.

Weird backgrounds, fonts, and logos.

Each of these is the website equivalent of bad wallpaper. No one wants to see it, touch it, or be around it. If something makes a website hard to read (or just plain hard to look at), then it probably isn't a great design feature.

If you have a website that displays one of these characteristics, then do us all a favor and get help today. As for the rest of us, it's our job to gently point the worst offenders in the right direction and bring them around to the light. After all, they might have bad websites, but we still have to look at them!

FAST RULES FOR YOUR DOMAIN NAME

When you name your company secure your domain name!

A good domain name adds credibility to your company but it also helps people remember you AND your website address. Would you rather do business with facemelter@yahoo.com or john@yourgraph.com? I think John sounds more professional, don't you?

Here are a few fast rules when purchasing a domain name:

1. **Get it as close to your company name or your own name as possible.** Get rid of all confusion and make sure people know who they are dealing with. After purchasing your name, set up your email account also.

2. **Spell it correctly.** I wonder how many people go to flicker.com rather than flickr.com? Make sure your website can be found!

3. **Make it easy to type.** You only have a few minutes to tell people about yourself, wasting time spelling out your domain name is not professional.

4. **Make it easy to remember.** "Hi, I'm Tammy, find me at WebServicesPeoria.com."

5. **Shorter is better.** If your company is a long complicated name, try to use an acronym for your website. Caterpillar Tractor Company is cat.com

6. **Avoid copyright infringement.** Think it through! I purchased MyPayPalCart.com to promote my PayPal Shopping carts. PayPal contacted me right away to make sure I knew I couldn't use the domain name. I wondered why it was available. I was out a little money but now know to think about my purchase rather than jumping in.

7. **Avoid numbers and letters that sounds like words.** WeWork4u. com is not the same as WeWorkForYou.com. So you will explain your domain name as "we, work, the number 4, the letter U dot com". That's just too confusing.

You will be able to purchase the perfect domain name at any of these companies.

- BuyTechTools.com

- GoDaddy.com

- Name.com

- 1and1.com

- NetworkSolutions.com

- Register.com

Be proactive when purchasing a domain name. If you already have a company even if you're not ready for website, get that company domain name.

The competition has been known to purchase domain names of their competitors. This is legal for them to do, so don't drag your feet when you're purchasing a domain name.

HOSTING YOUR WEBSITE

Website hosting is parking your domain name and website out on the Internet. All websites need a host. There are many hosting companies to choose from – some of you may have heard of GoDaddy or 1&1. They advertise heavily and are probably as good a company as any. When looking for a host for a small business site, it's a good idea to stay with someone reputable. Your business will rely on uptime, or the time your site is live. We should also keep in mind that it is imperative that your site be where it should be. It's difficult enough to get people to find your website than not be able to access it because of sloppy hosting. Ask the person building your site if they can recommend a host for you. Oftentimes, your website designer can host and manage your site also. Here are a few hosting companies that may be able to help you with your website:

- ◉ www.WebServicesInc.net

- ◉ www.BuyTechTools.com

- ◉ www.Godaddy.com

- ◉ www.EboundHost.com

- ◉ www.NetworkSolutions.com

Any of these hosting companies should do a nice job making sure your website is up and running.

Email Address

Once you have your domain name and hosting account setup, it's time to set up your email address. An email address with your company name adds credibility to your online presence. Even if it's something general such as info@yourcompany.com, this is a great way to show your professionalism.

Have an email address that matches your business. Your website should be using a good domain name (www.yourcompany.com) and an email address to match (info@yourcompany.com). This adds credibility. I remember working on a project with a person who's email address was facemelter@....com. My first impression was that he didn't know what he was doing. It was a development project with PHP for a company. I did the design work and FaceMelter did the development. About half way into the project I realized he was a very valuable asset and even hired him later to do more work for my company. I wonder how much work the developer had missed out on because of his email address. Do you want to do business with someone with an email address facemelter@......com? My point is: make your email professional and credible while making it easy for your clients to remember you.

CONTENT IS KING

Focus and precision are the keys to success.

Unless you have a Fortune 500 marketing budget, then you're wasting your time trying to reach too many different types of buyers and selling everything to everyone. In this economy and competitive landscape, it just doesn't work – it costs too much money to cast a wide net online, and even if you could, you'd be facing dozens or hundreds of niche competitors who want to steal your customers.

The answer, at least for most companies, has been to focus on specific types of buyers and products. Whether your customers all like a certain brand, fit a certain demographic, or live and work in a certain geographic area, identifying them closely (and then tailoring your marketing focus appropriately) is the key to success and a high return on investment. This trend will likely continue as more and more companies go online, so think now about where your profits are really coming from so you can target the right people effectively.

Time is just as important as money.

When the Internet was new, it created entirely different kinds of business models, ones that were predicated on nothing more than low, low prices. After all, if you could sell from a warehouse full of merchandise and find customers online, you could charge less than other retailers could – and customers were happy to seek you out to find those savings.

Now, the opposite is true. Most of us spend enough of our days on the Internet; we don't have lots of time to bargain-shop for anything but the most expensive purchases. That means that shorter web pages, less frequent e-mail newsletters, websites that are highly usable and searchable are all forms of convenience that your clients are willing to pay for. Treat their time the same way you would their money, and you'll discover that more of them will come back to you again and again.

Recommendations are all-important.

Economic experts like to say that the Internet has completely changed the way commerce works, even affecting things like the lifecycle of a small business. I don't think that's entirely true. It certainly seems as if strong businesses are still thriving and weak ones are being forced out of the market, but the whole process is just happening more quickly than it ever has before.

Here is why: When services and great products are worth the money being spent, or prices are too high, the Internet causes word to get out very, very quickly. And so, it takes less time for customers to find the really great vendors, and less time for them to weed out the ones who aren't worth spending money with. The bottom-line lesson? Reviews, recommendations, and reputations are all-important in the Internet age. Spend time cultivating positive word of mouth – especially on review sites and social media profiles – because they'll pay for themselves time and time again.

The art of Internet marketing is changing, and smart companies are changing right along with it. Are you following the three rules that dictate success now?

SEARCH ENGINE OPTIMIZATION

As we said before the domain name is important to search engines and having your company name as your domain name makes good sense. Please make sure that you have good page titles also. For example, rather than "about us" as your page title for your about us web page, call it "About Company ABC Peoria Illinois". Remember people usually include location when searching for local companies or services so add that in your title pages.

Of course making sure that you have great titles, descriptions, and keywords within your website is equally important. METADATA are the tags in the back end of your website. Go to any website and right click on the page, choose view source, and you can see what the data looks like. Another way to add keywords to your website is to add "alt" tags to your graphics. Alt tags are alternative tags or names of your pictures. People with disabilities that use your site will be the alternative listing of images rather than the images. You can use these tags with any picture within your website. Each time an alt tag is attached to a picture, this is just another way for someone to able to find your website. Use keywords within your website also.

Don't forget your body text and headings within your website! This is important for find-ability also. Try to look at your website as your visitors would. Think of how people would search for you on Google and try to incorporate those words within your website

Back Links

Approximately 80% of website visitors utilize search engines to find products, services and information. Having your website found on the Internet is just as important as it looking professional. Most people will agree that the best search engine optimization tool is back links. Back links are links back to your website. In other words, each mention back to your website is another street so people can come to your business. Back links can be characterized by social media links, links from articles, or links back from press releases. I always tell people to target natural organic a link structures. For instance, getting listed on directories is a great way to get these incoming links back to your website. Online directories are also a great way to get links back to your website. Simply do a Google search for "online directory" and your city name. You should get a listing of a few free online directories in your area that you can add your website to. In addition, asking people to link to your page is a great idea! Think of vendors or other people that you work with and simply ask them to link to your website.

Please be mindful of what websites you are linking to. One of my customers linked her website on adult friend finder, not knowing that it was an adult website. She got a lot of traffic all right, but it wasn't the traffic that she wanted. There are also companies that will offer to link your website to thousands of other websites. Bad links like this can result in black listing. Blacklisting is when a search engine will take your website out of their listings. To get back into the listing you have to prove that you have taking care of the problems. Unfortunately, that can sometimes take weeks.

- ◉ Here are some other ways that you can get blacklisted

- ◉ Invisible or hidden text on your pages

- ◉ Improper submission to search engines

- ◉ Keywords spamming or stuffing

- ◉ FFA – free for all sites. These are sites that are link farms sites built just for linking to other websites.

FREE WEBSITES?

Sometimes if you are on a budget, there are other options for building a website. If you are willing to build the website yourself, there are many other choices. Oftentimes, you can even get free hosting with your website. I will also tell you how to use your domain name with these sites. But first, let's talk about your options:

WordPress.com

WordPress.com used to be a blogging website but it's so much more than that! In fact, WordPress.com was elected best CMS (Content Management System) website a few years ago. When he accepted the award, the CEO said jokingly, "Don't tell anyone but we are a blog." WordPress.com has several hundred templates and you can add plugins for options such as shopping carts or online forms. With it's very user-friendly interface, it's very easy to add pages and administer your website. Your website address would be, for example:
http://yourcompany.wordpress.com

Wix.com

Wix.com is a website that enables you to drop and drag images to a screen to build your website. The interface is very visual and user-friendly. Keep in mind that the websites that you build here are Wix's sites. Your website would be, for example: http://wix.com/8900url

Weebly.com

Weebly.com is another site with drop and drag capabilities. Like the others, it's user-friendly.

A few things to keep in mind when building your own site:

1. For true ownership, have a website built for you by a professional. Since these sites are build on Wix, WordPress and Weebly platforms, the sites are theirs.

2. Search Engine Optimization is always an issue with these types of websites.

3. Do you really have time to build and manage your own website?

4. What happens if something goes wrong? Will you be able to diagnose the problem?

You can see that it would be difficult to tell anyone your domain name with these long web addresses from the free sites. This is why it's a good idea to point your domain name to these links. Here is how you do it: purchase your domain name through one of the registrars. Click the option for domain forwarding, and type in the long web address. Then, when someone types in your domain name, the domain will point to your long web address from the free sites.

QUALITY CUSTOMER SERVICE – KEY TO ONLINE WEBSITE SUCCESS

Providing quality online customer service is extremely important to the success of your business. Even if people truly want the product or service you are providing, they will go without if they receive unsatisfactory customer service. You have to go that extra mile when it comes to providing quality customer service online especially when competitors are ready to pounce on that jilted client.

A computer simply cannot provide the smile that means all the difference in face to face customer service. Therefore, you must take steps to optimize your website to make it more customer-friendly. Here are some tips for creating a customer-friendly website, which will help you to provide positive and high quality customer service:

Contact Information

People may need additional information regarding the product or service you offer. Provide contact information that is easily accessible. Make sure to include an address, phone number, fax number, and email address. Provide an actual link to your email address. If you have a location or store-front, Google Maps will allow you to place a map with driving directions on your website. This will enable clients to find you easily.

FAQ Page

A FAQ (frequently asked questions) page helps your customers find answers to their questions immediately without having to contact you. This is a very important page because it addresses the needs of the customer sometimes before they even realize they have a particular question.

The key to success is capturing your customer's attention before they leave your site. If you provide them with the answers they need to make an informed decision now, they will be more likely to stay on the page and possibly purchase the product/service you are selling.

Email Newsletter

Setting up an email newsletter is an essential tool for quality customer service. An email marketing system such as Constant Contact or a free program, MailChimp.com, is software that allows you to send emails each month to hundreds of clients at once without causing issues with your mail-host. You can create beautiful, eye-catching email from the hundreds of templates available with these programs. The best part of Email Marketing is the reporting tools.

Reporting tools within the email marketing programs can tell you who opened the email, what links were clicked on and if your email was forwarded to a friend. Why is this important? A great example can be: your email contains a link to register for a workshop you are giving. You see that someone had clicked the link but did not register for the workshop. You can contact that person via email and ask them if they had trouble registering or if they would like a coupon for the workshop. By seeing the client clicked the link, you know the interest is there.

Video "How-tos" or Testimonials

Video is very popular online these days. Many spas and salons can get a great customer connection with how-to videos. For instance, a video to demonstrate proper methods for hair care can be much for convincing than an article to read. Why not end the video with links to products featured that were used in the video for easy sales?

Do you have clients who love you? Why not make a video of their testimonial so others can see it. YouTube (www.youtube.com) will allow you to post these videos for free and also give you a link to embed on your website. YouTube boasts 1 billion views per day on their website so the chances of your video being seen are very good!

Feedback

Ask customers to communicate with you through feedback. People feel that if they are given the opportunity to communicate through feedback, even if it is negative, then they can trust your company. Make communication easy for clients by using social media such as Facebook for that instant feedback. And most importantly, follow up with your clients after they leave feedback.

These simple strategies can help you provide the customer service your potential clients need to give them that extra bit of security when trying to make a decision on whether to buy from you or another company.

HOW A GOOD ONLINE STORE IS LIKE AN NFL PLAYOFF TEAM

It's that time of the year again, where we anxiously watch insanely huge millionaires slam into each other for the right to come back and do it again for another weekend... and naturally, to think about how that relates to e-commerce and online stores.

Believe it or not, there are actually some pretty good comparisons between the two. In fact, in a lot of ways, a good online store is quite a bit like an NFL playoff team.

Here's why: Just as with football, it's important to have at least one or two strengths over your competitors. These are the "difference makers" on offense and defense, the ones who can change the game. When it comes to an online store, these could be things like better prices, longer-lasting products, or a searchable catalog.

Also like football, however, it's important to remember that even though these advantages are necessary, they aren't enough to guarantee you success. Think of all the superstar players who never won a Super Bowl ring, the great ones who didn't have a strong enough supporting cast to get it done.

There are really good online stores that fail for the same reasons – they do some things really well, but can't leverage those strengths because they have too many other weaknesses. If you have an online store, or are thinking about starting one, here are a few things you can't consistently turn a profit without:

A unique domain name.

If people have to struggle to remember where to find you online, then there's a very good chance they won't. After a few minutes of frustration, they'll just click elsewhere.

A good search engine optimization plan.

You have to have visitors to your website before you can have buyers for your products, and more than 85% of all visits to online stores start with sites like Google. Remember to set up your Google Places page. These pages usually come up first when searching by location. It's free!

A strategy for following up with buyers frequently.

If you aren't on the top of your buyers' mind, then someone else probably is. Why keep working to attract customers when it's easier to keep the ones you have? Email marketing and social media are great ways to do this.

Strong customer service.

In the same way, your reputation is everything online. If buyers feel like they aren't getting a good deal, or good service, from your business, then it's only a matter of time before they tell a few hundred thousand of their closest friends on Twitter, Facebook, and elsewhere.

As with playoff football, running an online store seems a lot easier when you're watching someone else do it. If you think you're ready to get into the game, and want to play to win, remember that e-commerce success takes the right mixture of superstar advantages and supporting details. You'll have to get both right if you want to win new sales.

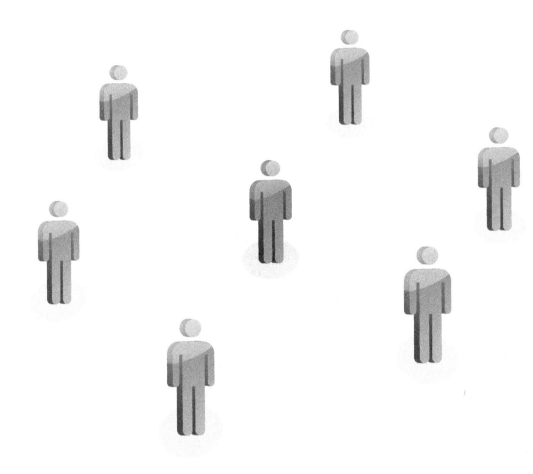

Section Four
INTERNET MARKETING

REVIEWS : ONE THING THAT MUST BE A PART OF EVERY ONLINE MARKETING PLAN

Although I spend a good deal of my time giving advice to business owners, managers, and executives on getting the most from Internet marketing – usually through seminars, consulting packages, or articles like this one – I never really like to give out hard and fast rules.

The reason is simple: Things change on the web so quickly that each situation could be different. It is impossible to say that a certain piece of advice is going to be applicable for everyone for every situation. I am going to break my rule today and offer one rule that every small business should keep in mind.

You must absolutely make online reviews part of your Internet marketing plan.

What makes this particular piece of advice so compelling? There are a few reasons that Internet reviews matter, but we'll focus on two in particular. First, reviews on the major sites tend to show up very high in the search engine rankings. They are incredibly easy for your current and potential customers to find. Second, they represent the very best of word-of-mouth advertising – probably the oldest and best-known way to grow your company, online or off.

With that in mind, here are a few tips for making the most of my rule and making online reviews a big part of your marketing plan:

Know the major review sites in your industry.

There are many review sites out there, but not all of them are important to you. While a dentist might need to pay the most attention to Yelp, for example. Restaurants and Hotels should focus their attention on TripAdvisor. Figure out what your customers are reading, and then add a profile for your business if you need to.

Monitor what others are saying about you, your products, and your service.

It does not take very much time to check for new reviews, but it is a step many business owners and managers skip. A single poor review can heavily impact your business. So, take a few minutes each week, mark it on your calendar if you have to and go to these sites to see what has been posted about your business. You should also check and see what others are saying about your competitors in the area.

Respond to questions quickly and clearly.

Customers will go to these sites to openly ask a question about your business. When they do, feel free to respond publicly, with all the detail that is needed (provided that you aren't sharing sensitive contact or account info). Other potential buyers might have had the same question, so it is a great way to address many people at once.

Handle complaints delicately.

Your first instinct when reading a poor review might be to get angry, or to reply with a ranting message. Resist the urge! Instead, find out what happened, see if you can pacify the disappointed buyer, and post a reasoned-out public reply if it seems appropriate.

I recently read an article about a bakery who posted a picture of a crying baby in response to a bad complaint on a review site. We can all agree that the customer isn't always right, but making things right with your customers goes a long way. Looking back, I bet the bakery wished they handled the customer's response differently, especially after the story was picked up by several national news outlets. Handling this complaint this way seems to verify that she was rude and childish to the customer when she complained in person. Managing complaints with dignity and professionalism is key to good business practices. Making it right with your customers should be priority.

Of course, know that some people can't be pleased... know when to simply call it a day and move on to the next customer.

Do everything you can to encourage positive reviews.

The more positive reviews you have, the more new customers can trust you, and the faster your business can grow. You never want to do anything unethical (like trading services for positive reviews), but don't be afraid to let good customers know that reviews are important, and ask them to share a few kind words online. Why not have a list of review sites available at your store or have a list of review site links on your website?

With the right reviews in the right places, you could see the profitability of your company double or even triple in a short amount of time. For that to happen, though, you need to follow these steps and be sure that the great work you do is being noted on review sites in your area.

Be a good customer.

On the flip side of this topic is **you or your business** being a good customer. Each time you write a nice review about a business or one of your vendors, your name is attached to it for years. The business or vendor may share your comments with their audience getting your name out in front of even more people. If you were to Google "Tammy Finch", your search results would not only belong to my website and social media pages, but many of my reviews of books and equipment that I've purchased as well as hotel and restaurant recommendations. Writing reviews are almost as effective as getting them. Keep that in mind and try to get in the habit of being a good customers and sharing good experiences with the masses.

How is your doctor's service? I bet he would appreciate your kind words on Google's local review site. Did the waiter stand out at your favorite restaurant? Tell people about it! An attendee at one of my social media workshops said his business took off after someone wrote a nice review on Angie's List. One review and his business is going full-force. He was a true believer of social media and online word of mouth marketing.

Here are some links to some important review sites. Set up an account and claim your listing.

- ◉ Yelp.com

- ◉ Google Places and Yahoo Local

- ◉ TripAdvisor.com

- ◉ InsiderPages.com

- ◉ Local.com

- ◉ AngiesList.com

- ◉ MerchantCircle.com

- ◉ CitySearch.com

- ◉ UrbanSpoon.com

FOUR STEPS TO INTRODUCING YOURSELF TO A BUSINESS CONTACT ONLINE

There is an old saying that, in business, it isn't what you know but who you know. While we could spend hours debating the truth or wisdom of that statement, the reality is that we all know that it gets a lot easier to accomplish your professional goals when you're running in the right circles. In other words, it might not be all about who you know, but it certainly matters.

That would be a great piece of insight, if it weren't for all the hard work that goes into getting to know the right people. Finding ways to introduce yourself to key contacts is a challenge that is practically as old as time itself, and without any can't-miss answers... or at least it was until now.

Here is why: Introducing yourself to an unknown VIP at a business event, or picking up the phone and making a cold call, can be a stressful event with a low probability for success. And there isn't any guarantee you have someone in your existing network who can make the introduction, so gaining a referral can be difficult. Since those used to be the only options, however, you just had to live with them. Now, though, times have changed – smart businessmen and women can use tools like social media to make online introductions a lot faster, simpler, and more profitable.

If that sounds good to you, then here are some easy steps to follow to introduce yourself to someone important online:

Step 1. Do your homework.

It isn't enough to know who you want to meet, you also have to know why they should want to meet you. It's also a good idea to know a bit more about them than their title or alma mater. Use Google, LinkedIn, and the other tools at your fingertips to form a more complete profile of your contact, and don't stop until you feel certain you could have a good conversation with them about their work or professional interests.

Step 2. Look for mutual acquaintances.

In some cases, you may find that the two of you already have a number of contacts in common, which makes your introduction a lot easier. If you don't, however, then consider making those intermediary introductions first. Often, it's easier and smarter to meet the person who is close to the customer or mentor you want to have before approaching them directly.

Step 3. Reach out non-aggressively.

It's amazing how many people still treat e-mail and social media like a seedy night club, desperate to chat up a new contact and rub up against them (virtually speaking) way too soon. Remember that, as important as this introduction might be to you, your contact has other things going on in his or her life and career – don't come on too strong or ask for too much of their time right away. Simply introduce yourself, mention why you would like to meet them, and then take the next step...

Step 4. Follow-up via mail, phone call, or face-to-face contact.

What that next step means depends largely on you, your location, and the business goal you are hoping to meet. Still, social media and other forms of online communication can't replace more personal forms of contact, so try to further the relationship off-line if possible.

The Internet has made introducing yourself to new people easier, but that doesn't mean you should rush out to touch base with every professional you want to work with. Follow these steps, and you'll come across as a lot more informed, not to mention a little more polished. Once you accomplish that, you'll be well on the way to reaching your goal!

HOW TO BE A BETTER DIGITAL CITIZEN

Most of us would agree that "being a good citizen" is an easy way to make the world a better place, and part of our unspoken, unsigned contract with the rest of society. We count on each other to do things like be polite to strangers, pick up after ourselves in public parks, and even let another driver cut in front of us from time to time... it's how we do our part to keep things moving along.

As the world becomes more and more digital, however, maybe it's time for all of us to start thinking about what we can do to be better digital citizens, as well. After all, many of us "see" more people online in an average day than we ever do on the street. And, the way we treat each other on the web can make a big difference in our time, mood, and productivity.

With that in mind, here are five things I think we can do to become better digital citizens. I hope you'll give them a try – or better yet, share some other suggestions of your own:

1. Think before you forward things.

Unwanted e-mails have become a modern form of the chain letter, clogging up our inboxes and taking up too much of our time. If you have contacts on your list that you suspect might not find pictures of cats as amusing as you do, either ask them outright or trim them from your list.

2. Don't tag others and photos without warning.

So, you decide to scan all of those old pictures and post them to Facebook. That's great, but make sure the people who are also in your photos want them going online, too, especially if they could be embarrassing. As we get older, some of us don't want the whole world remembering the "fun" decisions we made when we were younger, especially if they could impact marriages, careers, etc.

3. Be respectful.

One of the strangest things about the Internet is its tendency to bring people together in a way that is either completely anonymous, or close to it. Without the intricacies of face-to-face contact (or the risk of getting punched in the face), a lot of people are bolder and more aggressive with their opinions than they would be otherwise. We can all be a little nicer online, and a little more respectful of other people's ideas, and the world would be a better place for it.

4. Share what's cool.

There are lots of reasons to surf the Internet, but one of the best is the possibility of coming across something really great, even though you weren't looking for it. When you share awesome things (like recipes, jokes, or fun stories you have found), you help create that joy for someone else. Just remember what we've already said and don't forward them constantly unless you've been invited to do so.

5. Write good reviews.

There are a lot of scams and bad ideas out there, so why not award people, companies, and vendors for doing something great for you? Now more than ever, small businesses rely on positive feedback from customers to build a strong reputation and let people know that they'll do what they say they will. Writing positive reviews lets you help the growing businesses that deserve it, while steering other customers towards the bargains and values that are out there to be found.

The world's getting bigger, and the Internet is making it smaller at the same time. If we all practiced being better digital citizens, then imagine what we could accomplish online!

LEARN THE INS AND OUTS OF EMAIL MARKETING

Have you ever thought of email marketing to help improve your business and connect with clients? Email marketing is a great way to keep in contact with clients and share valuable information with them. Believe it or not, your clients are interested in your company and want to know the latest news in your industry or community.

Your emails should contain information that is interesting to your clients. Provide them with short paragraphs about articles or website information, and link back to the full article to keep their interest. Sending emails with sales pitches may turn customers off.

Your customers want to connect with you but on their terms. Give them options for signing up for your email newsletter, social media accounts or just providing your email address and phone number, and let them choose how they connect.

Being flexible is important to your clients. I prefer email, but I am fine with signing up with newsletters as long as they are short and full of information. Providing valuable information makes you the expert in your field. It is important to build customer confidence and credibility.

A few tips for Email Marketing:

Always use an email marketing program like Constant Contact or MailChimp. Not only do the emails look attractive, but clients have an option to opt in or out of your list.

Check your reporting tools of the program to see what your clients are interested in. Who opened the file and what did they click on?

Use short bursts of information and link back to your website. This drives more traffic to your site but also keeps the reader's attention.

Easy and efficient email marketing is within your reach. Well designed email marketing can increase your customer base and grow your sales. If you are interested in Email marketing, feel free to attend one of my free workshops for Constant Contact. Check my website for a schedule. www.WebServicesInc.net.

TIPS FOR INCREASING YOUR EMAIL MARKETING LIST

Are you seeing positive results from your email marketing strategies? Do you want to utilize email marketing but have no idea where to begin? Here are a few tips for increasing your mail list and subsequently increasing your customer base.

If you are using Constant Contact as your email marketing program, use their free app on Facebook "Join my list". All you have to do is join the app page on Facebook and add the email address from your Constant Contact. This way clients can sign up for your newsletter right from your Facebook page. It is important to allow your customers to connect with you on their terms.

If you have a store front, post a sign in your store showing your social media accounts and text keyword to join your email list. Who knows, someone may just use their smart phone to connect with you immediately. Small postcards with this information can also be placed in their bags to look at later.

Don't forget your email signature. Let your customers know you have a monthly newsletter or coupons. Make sure when clients sign up, they know exactly how often they will receive the emails.

Most people think having your email waiting for people first thing in the morning is a great idea. Is it? Sorting through email first thing in the morning, news may get missed. Why not try sending it around 10am or so after the morning email is sorted? Try it and see if your open rate increases by using your reporting tools.

Use a good subject line to increase open rates. Just saying "news from company ABC" is not good enough. How about something like "Increase your Revenue with these Quick Tips". Let people know they are about to open something valuable.

Email marketing is a great way to keep in contact with clients. It's a cost effective way to keep your "face" in front of your clients and potential clients.

If you want to try it for a month, sign up for a FREE trial at my website http://webservicesinc.net/resources.html

WHAT EXACTLY IS GOOGLE IMPLYING?

Although you might not have noticed – most people haven't – Google recently added another search tab to its advanced features: the ability to filter sites by their reading level. It's an interesting idea, and one that was probably inevitable in this age of bad grammar and the text-type shortcuts we've all gotten used to sending each other over the past few years.

Still, the idea that the world's largest search engine is making determinations about how hard something is or isn't to read is an interesting development. It also raises all kinds of little issues that could ultimately affect the future of the web's strange ways.

For one thing, this presumably means that search engine spiders are now looking at content slightly differently, figuring out how many SAT words you have on each page, how long your paragraphs are, what kinds of subjects you are working with, etc. And for another, it sort of implies that most of us either can't or won't read websites that take us beyond the level of familiarity with the dictionary we would need to read the sports section, for example.

This might have implications that are both useful and harmful, but here are a few we should consider:

The Internet may start to resemble old newsstands.

Although you don't see as many of them around anymore, you'll notice something interesting if you take a look at the newsstands on busy city streets, or in the airports. Namely, you'll see that magazines aren't just sorted by different interests, but also grouped in a way that makes it easy for you to pick out the reading level you are looking for. Could the same thing eventually happen on the Internet? It probably already does, in an informal way, but we may start to see more of a formal divide between "everyday" websites and more "intellectual" destinations.

The quality of writing you put online is more important than ever.

A lot of people blame blogs, along with texting, for the lower and lower standards that we apply to the English language these days. That might not be a terrible thing – after all, more of us are communicating more clearly than ever – but it has also led most of us to subconsciously judge the writing we see based on things like spelling and grammar. How long before Google and the other major search engines start to heavily penalize you for certain kinds of errors? The quality of writing you put on your blog, website, and social networks is going to become more important than ever.

We could all probably pay more attention to the basics of language.

Even for those of us who don't write – on the Internet or elsewhere – it might be a good idea to start brushing up on our grammar and punctuation. While no one enjoys thinking about things like nouns and verbs, the fact of the matter is that they let us be precise in explaining our ideas to other people. That's an underrated benefit, even in the digital age.

When you get to the bottom of it, Google is really just telling us something we already know by adding reading level filters to its search results: that some users just don't want to read big words. That's understandable, but it says a lot more about us than it does the world's most popular search engine.

ARE YOU USING YOUR SMART PHONE FOR GOOD, OR EVIL?

In the interest of full disclosure, I should probably admit that I used a headline that might be slightly over the top. But, while most of us probably aren't using our iPhones, Androids, and other smart phones for purely evil purposes, we probably aren't using them for as much good as we could be, either.

Don't worry, I'm not writing to tell you about a superhero app that compels you to fight crime. What I'm actually getting at is the fact that many of us first upgraded to web-ready devices to get more done, which is certainly a fine and achievable goal. What ends up happening, however, is that they end up wasting as much time for us as they save.

Regular readers of my column will know I'm all about efficiency and productivity. So, I recently asked myself: How can we all start using our smart phones for better effect and get more of our money's worth from our monthly plans?

After racking my brain, searching the Internet, and seeing what some leading experts have to say on the topic, here are my best tips:

Think carefully before you buy or download an app.

Apple wasn't lying when they promised "there is an app for that." Our smart phones can literally do more now than NASA could just decades ago. That's not all good news, though, because it can tempt us to download lots of apps – especially games and other useless items – that we don't need, or necessarily even want.

Put yourself on two important budgets.

That phenomenon of "downloading just because it's there" leads us to an important point. You need to put yourself on two different budgets: one for time, and another for money. How much are you spending on your smart phone, in terms of dollars and the precious minutes of your life? Find the right level for both, and then stick to your "budget" every day.

Recognize the signs that you have a smart phone problem.

Although very few people actually have an "addiction" to smart phones the way they do to alcohol or drugs, relying too much on mobile technology can hurt the relationships you have with other people. If others are always annoyed with you because of your phone usage, or your tendency to check e-mail on your cell phone is putting your job in jeopardy, then it's time to get serious about cutting back.

Think twice about that upgrade.

Although it's always great to have the latest device, the hard truth is that most new "upgrades" have a lot more to do with marketing than they do actual mobile communication capabilities. There may be better things to spend your time and money on than the latest phone, so be sure to keep your priorities in balance.

Keeping these little pieces of advice in mind can help you make the most of your smart phone, and stop you from wasting time and money month after month. Of course, if you have your own tips to share, I'd love to hear them. E-mail me today and let me know what you think!

THE THREE THINGS YOU CAN LEARN FROM THE WEB DEVELOPMENT TEAM AT CHASE BANK

When Chase Bank customers recently lost access to their accounts, it caused a bit of an uproar, online and off. Apparently it's one thing for users to go without their banking balances and other details during scheduled maintenance, in the rare hours of a Tuesday morning... and it's quite another for Monday to start without access to the things they're looking for.

I'm not trying to pick on Chase for whatever caused their problems (these things happen), but there are three important lessons that every person and business should learn from their latest fiasco:

1. **You have to be prepared for short outages with technology.**

Software, hardware, and even the electrical grid can all fail from time to time, and there is really no excuse for being unprepared. That's especially true with a major international bank, whose clients depend on steady, reliable access to their accounts. It also applies to the rest of us, however, since most of us are also dependent on technology in numerous different ways.

Remember that different parts of your hardware and software setup – and especially hard drives and servers – give out at small but predictable rates. Have a backup plan for each of them, so that the loss wouldn't leave you "stranded," technologically speaking.

2. Make sure your customers can get access to what they need.

Chase, like all major banks, has a telephone backup system to deal with emergencies. That might not please every customer, but it does help to limit the damage, and prevents them from having liability issues down the road. That is, if someone really needed to get access to their money, all they had to do is pick up the closest phone.

If you own a business, or just work for one, that's something worth thinking about. It isn't entirely uncommon to hear from a customer service representative that they can't help you because "systems are down," or that "e-mail is unavailable." That's not good enough, especially if it's for extended periods of time. While there might not be millions of dollars riding on your customers being able to do what they need to, the future of your business might be, so have backup systems in place.

3. Pent-up frustration usually comes out online.

The most interesting thing about the Internet outage at Chase wasn't just that customers immediately took to Twitter and other social media sites to vent their frustrations, but that they did so with an extreme amount of anger and venom. In fact, the reactions seemed a bit extreme, given that most were simply annoyed that they couldn't check balances and cleared payments.

You don't have to read far between the lines to see that these weren't the biggest frustrations of all. Customers were simply mad at having one more annoyance – starting with extra fees for things like ATMs and debit cards. In other words, they were simply venting existing frustration in a new direction. The point? If your business isn't doing a good job of taking care of people in other areas, then they'll use a simple technical failure (or almost any other kind of challenge) as an excuse to use your brand for a punching bag online.

For most people, managing a multi-billion-dollar enterprise, and the accompanying web technology, isn't a big problem for them. That doesn't mean you shouldn't be learning from the example Chase is setting, though. Think about what happened to them in just a few hours off-line, and what your company could do to avoid the same.

SEVEN PAY PER CLICK TIPS – THE POWERS OF PPC

Pay per Click (PPC) is an Internet marketing tool used on search engines and content sites, such as blogs. To use PPC, advertisers pay their host when an ad is clicked on. PPC ads display an advertisement that matches an advertiser's keyword list. These ads are placed on websites that choose to host specific ads. With search engines, advertisers bid on keyword phrases that are relevant to their target market. With content sites, there is generally a fixed price per click instead of a bidding system.

In a flat rate PPC, the advertiser and publisher agree on a fixed amount to be paid for each click. The publisher will have a rate card that lists the cost per click that is used within different areas of the website or network. While this is a guideline, advertisers have the option of negotiating lower rates, especially if there is a long-term or high-value contract involved.

Seven Tips for an Effective PPC Campaign

Step 1. Determine your Goals. Decide on a strategy on how to reach these goals.

Step 2. Make Informed Decisions. Gather data that is not limited to one single online source. Find other sources to enhance your options. Do not just go with the "latest trend", as you can be missing out on a profitable source.

Step 3. Track Keywords with a Keyword Tool Key. There are a few places to find the keywords that are the most valuable. Make use of these to ensure you are tracking the right keywords that will be profitable to your PPC campaign.

Step 4. It's Quality rather than Quantity. Bid on keywords relevant to your website. Therefore, do not just bid on any and all keywords. This may drive a lot of traffic to your site, but will not produce the results you want, if they are not keywords relevant to your website. Start with a group of base keywords related to your site and expand on those. This is an ongoing process that must be reviewed on a consistent basis.

Step 5. Landing Pages are Important in PPC. Avoid flashy images, videos or bright colors on your landing pages. Make sure they are focused on getting the user to do what you want them to do. Make sure the "order now" or "add to cart" button is easy to see.

Step 6. Avoid Signing up with every PPC Program. There are a lot of PPC programs available, but they may not have the tools you need to help you operate an efficient PPC campaign. Yahoo, MSN, Ask, and Google are the ones to use! They will offer the most for your return on investment.

Step 7. Create Campaigns with the Seasons. Schedule your campaigns around the upcoming holidays or seasons. Use holiday terms or seasons, such as Christmas gifts or Spring Lawn Care. More people are out there looking for these types of items or services during specific times of the year.

An effective PPC campaign can help users become more familiar with your website. Once they develop a sense of trust with the content on your site, they are more likely to come back, which will help you with the rankings in search engines. While it is a goal to get as many people as possible to visit your site, remember it is even more important to get credible users who could become potential profitable clients or customers. Otherwise you are paying for clicks that will not lead to positive results.

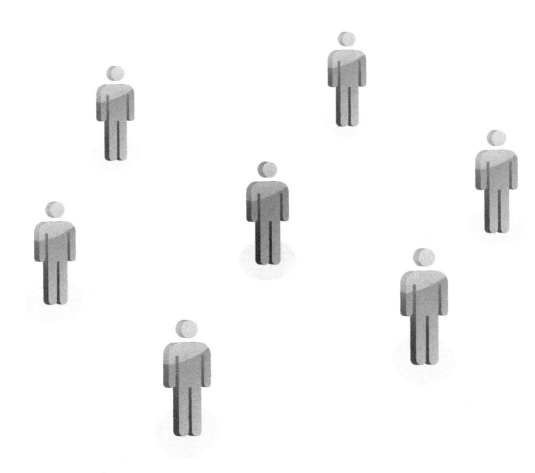

Section Five

YOUR COMPUTER AND YOU

5 GOLDEN RULES FOR THE TECHNOLOGY AGE

Is technology making our lives easier? Economists and retailers would insist that it absolutely is, and they're probably right, although it's hard to feel that way when you're one blue screen error away from taking a chainsaw to your laptop.

The point is that computers can be wonderful tools, but they can also be incredibly frustrating when we either aren't using them correctly, or they do things that we didn't expect them to.

Even though I'm firmly on the humans' side when it comes to our love-hate relationship with technology, I have to admit that there are certain things we do that make our technological lives harder than they have to be. That's because there are some problems and situations that are either completely predictable (when you stop to think about them), or simply come about because we don't establish the right working habits.

In order to show you what I mean – and hopefully make all of your lives a lot easier in the process – here are my five golden rules for the technology age:

1. Know your technology.

Here is a quick pop quiz: How many hours per day do you spend using your computer, smart phone, etc.? And how many minutes did you spend looking at the manual?

If you are like most of us, there is a pretty enormous disconnect between those two amounts of time. And yet, the number one problem with most forms of technology is user error, plain and simple. The more you know about your technology, the easier it is to use it. If you aren't into reading manuals (and who is?), check out an advice forum or a YouTube video. What you learn could make your life a lot easier.

2. Back up everything.

Every once in a while, you read a story about repairs being made to a space shuttle or orbiting satellite. That's a pretty startling indictment of technology, if you think about it: If the geniuses at NASA can't make technology error-proof, then what chance does the hardware and software you use have?

Your computers (and especially things like hard drives) are eventually going to fail – you can count on it. With that in mind, it makes great sense to back up all your work files, personal photos, and other information on a regular basis. I've seen more than a few people cry over lost wedding pictures, Quickbooks files and school documents. Here is a good place to start: Carbonite Online Back up http://www.carbonite.com.

3. Use your Internet time wisely.

The Internet has gotten to be so big that you could easily lose entire weeks every year surfing through things that are fun, but ultimately not that useful to your life (a phenomenon I've written about before).

That means it's getting harder and harder – and more and more important – to ration the time you spend online. Treat it like TV or any other form of amusement, and make sure you aren't giving it more of your attention than it deserves.

4. Treat the Internet like a time capsule.

Speaking of the Internet, it isn't just about how you spend your time, but also what you post. Remember that the things you put online (and especially social media sites) could be around on a scale of time that borders on "forever."

Things that are embarrassing, damaging to your career, or harmful to current and future relationships are best kept off-line, not on Facebook where they'll still be haunting you two or three decades from now.

5. Ignore technology once in a while.

Even when it's working really well, technology is no substitute for friends, family, and the other things we love. It doesn't matter if you make your living with computers (as I do), make a point of getting away from them once in a while. You'll find that you'll appreciate them a lot more when you come back, not to mention having a more fun and fulfilling life!

FIVE TIPS FOR USING THE INTERNET MORE PRODUCTIVELY

The Internet is a great tool for work and research, but it can easily become a time-waster as well. What starts out as a quick research session or work activity can quickly turn into hours spent watching YouTube videos of cats wearing suits and office pranks. And that's to say nothing of social media and e-mail, each of which can wreck the plans you made for your workday.

As much fun as those diversions might be, they probably aren't very good for the future of your career, not to mention your checking account. With that in mind, here are some tips to help you get some of your calendar back:

1. Don't go online for just one thing.

When was the last time you ever really just went on the Internet for 5 minutes? It usually takes longer than that just to check your e-mails. And even if you don't become distracted by web surfing, there is also the added time it will take you to come back and concentrate on what you were doing before.

The answer? Batch your Internet tasks (like reading industry websites or checking your e-mail) together and do them all at once, or at least at regular times. It's a lot more efficient to go online three times a day for half an hour then it is to deal with the Internet 10 minutes at a time while trying to get other things done.

2. Make a shopping list before you leave your home page.

At least when you're working, you should try to avoid going onto the Internet without any clear purpose in mind. Just as going to the store without a shopping list is likely to leave you with a cart full of junk food, opening your browser with no destination in sight is a great way to kill your productivity.

Try writing down a list of the key facts or details you're looking for before you go online, and then close your browser once you've found them. That will save you time and keep you more focused.

3. Buy an egg timer.

One of the interesting things about using the Internet is that it's a lot like watching television – a few minutes can turn into a few hours before you know it, you are watching talking dog videos or looking at pictures of kids you don't even know. But, since you have other things to be working on, try keeping an egg timer, close by when you go online and race against the sand to get your tasks done.

By setting a time limit beforehand, you'll reduce your temptation to click every link you see. At the very least, you'll start to develop an understanding of how much time you're spending online.

4. Put certain sites off-limits.

If you have kids, then you're probably already familiar with all kinds of parental control software that blocks off certain types of pages from young impressionable eyes. Why not give yourself a taste of your own medicine? If you know that logging on to Facebook and Twitter, for example, is going to kill your day, then why not make them off-limits?

There are a number of free and easy-to-use software tools that can help you manage your Internet usage, and even set time limits on certain sites. Give one a try, and you might be surprised at the results.

5. Create an organizational system.

Have you ever found yourself researching the same question half a dozen times, or burning through an hour looking for that one web resource that seemed so perfect when you first found it? If so, then you already know why a good organizational system can be so important.

Just as with the files in your office, you should have a way to look up e-mails, bookmarked websites, and other online information later on. It might take you a day or two to learn how to sort them, but it's a skill that will pay you back time and time again.

Wasting time on the Internet is fun, but you don't want to let it eat so far into your productivity that your career starts to suffer. Use these tips to balance your online time, and you'll be well on the way to reclaiming a bit of your schedule.

COULD YOUR NEXT PART-TIME JOB BE ONLINE?

A lot of us wouldn't mind having a few extra dollars lying around, and have heard of making money from the Internet, but don't have the kind of technological genius that it takes to invent the next Facebook or Google. But did you know there are a number of ways that you could earn a bit of money on the Internet that don't involve learning things like computer programming?

Here are just a few of the ways people like you are making a bit of extra money here and there from the Internet:

Start a blog.

Blogging might not seem like a great way to make money, and in truth a lot of blogs aren't that profitable. Still, if you can write regular, informative articles on a topic you care about, it's a good bet you can develop a following over time – one that might click on some relevant ads, visit an online store you recommend, or even leave a few dollars in your virtual "tip jar."

Launch a simple online store.

You don't have to dream up the next Amazon.com to make money in e-commerce. In fact, it's usually easier to build a profitable online store if you think smaller and aim your products at a well-defined niche market. Don't let the fear of website design and programming hold you back, either; there are a number of low-cost services you can use to design your online store, upload product descriptions, and even accept credit cards and other payments without knowing anything about HTML.

Go on project sites like Elance.

Do you have a skill (like proofreading, library research, or data entry) that you could provide on a project basis? Visit a site like Elance.com and check out the postings by employers, and you might just be surprised at how many different jobs you could do, not to mention the money that's available. Whether you are looking to transition into full-time contract employment or simply earn a few extra dollars, the opportunities are virtually endless.

Launch a freelance business.

Of course, you don't have to work through sites like Elance to become a full-fledged freelancer. You could moonlight as a photographer, designer, or virtual assistant, for example, by simply setting up a website and a few online ads. Freelance work – especially when combined with regular employment – can be a great way to earn extra money on the side.

Write an e-book.

For a lot of people, the idea of writing tens of thousands of words brings back painful memories of their school days. So why would you want to consider writing an e-book or other informational product? The answer is simple: because writing isn't just more fun when you like the topics involved, but it can be a great way to earn a bit of extra money. To launch a successful e-book, think of specialized topics: What do you know that others would pay good money to learn about?

Are there other ways to make part-time money online? Absolutely. One thing each of these opportunities has in common, however, is that they cost very little to get started with, don't require a huge time commitment, and can potentially help you to earn hundreds of dollars or more every week.

So, if you've been thinking about saving a bit extra for your retirement, putting a few dollars aside for your children's education, or even just saving up for that dream car or special vacation, then giving yourself a part-time Internet job could be the answer. I hope you'll give it a try, and even better yet, write back and let me know about your success!

COULD YOUR NEXT PART-TIME JOB BE ONLINE? – PART 2

After my blog post last week about a part-time online job, I read several tweets and emails in response. I thought I would expand with a few more realistic ideas and suggestions.

Here are just a few more ways people like you are making a bit of extra money here and there from the Internet:

Sell your books, DVDs, and Games on Amazon.

I have an ongoing product list on Amazon, selling old CDs, PS2 games we don't play anymore and books that I've read. It doesn't cost anything to list them and buyers have to pay for shipping. Textbooks do not last long in the selling queue. Sometimes people will settle for older editions or they just want to learn on their own.

Launch a simple online store.

I wanted to expand on this. Using a PayPal shopping cart to sell your items online is a great option. No monthly credit card fees, selling items as you go or just directing people to the site once you run out of inventory at craft shows. Sites like http://craftycarts.com/ will make you a site for around $200.

Go on project sites like Freelancer.com for help.

My new friends at Freelancer.com gave me a better idea than being a freelancer, hiring one! Do you have an idea that you KNOW will be a money maker but can't afford to hire staff? Sites like Freelancer.com will enable you to find that perfect "employee" to hire for your one time project.

Write an e-book or app for Kindle.

Or better yet, hire a ghost writer or app developer to write it for you. I downloaded a simple app for my kindle called My Yoga Studio by Nickelbuddy to use when I travel. The app was $1.99. Nickelbuddy is smart to keep these apps cheap. Once it's developed, it is just a matter of marketing.

So, hopefully these ideas in conjunction with the previous ideas, will inspire an scheme for your next online job.

ONLINE SECURITY FOR THE PEOPLE

I was recently presenting at a workshop and a lady asked how to get off the Facebook list. I wasn't sure what she meant, so she told me she had received an email from Facebook that said her husband added pictures. She was asked to login through a link in an email. I knew right away it was a scam and told her to login to Facebook and change her password.

We have also had a few people come into Web Tech (our computer repair store) that said a popup window on their computer said their anti-virus license had expired. The pop-up window asked for a credit card and the customer gave it to them, 3 times!

There are also fake screens the take total control of your computer saying they are from the FBI or local government and that people need to pay right away.

Then, I read in the paper of someone who said their grandson called and he sent him money. It wasn't his grandson but someone pretending to be and it worked.

There are so many ways that people can get tricked into giving out personal information, passwords or even money. It's not just the elderly, my daughter was tricked by text message saying she won a gift card.

I thought I would put together a few tips on ways to dodge some of these scams.

1. Know what scammers are after:

Credit card information, social security number, date of birth, mother's maiden name. Don't give out this information to anyone.

2. Ask questions.

If someone calls you, ask your "grandson" what his mother's middle name is.

3. Pop-up windows or fake screens

that show up on your computer may ask for your credit card to renew something but if you are not sure, call for help. Chris at Web Tech Services in East Peoria will answer quick questions for free at 309-699-9327.

4. Use common sense.

If it sounds too good to be true, it probably is.

5. Email with links should not be clicked.

Go to your internet browser and go directly to the website and login.

6. Email stating that you have a package coming soon

from any of the shipping companies are often fake and ridden with email links that attempt to install malware on your computer.

If your email or social network has been compromised, first login and change your password. Make it something difficult. Adding symbols, capital letters and numbers make your password more difficult to obtain. Pick a word or name and add these codes to it.

For example: Difficult can be D!fF1culT – you can remember this word. And using exclamation points and numbers in place of letters they look like will help you remember. Zeros for O's, number one for L's and @ for A's are just a few. Get creative because your security may depend on it.

I am working on a free workshop for local community groups to show samples of some of these scams and how to help you become more aware. I will keep you posted. For now, be careful out there! As always use common sense, if it sounds shady, it probably is!

COULD "DO NOT CALL" BE COMING TO YOUR COMPUTER?

As far as laws go, the bill that created the national "do not call" registry was a clear winner, giving people an easy way out of being interrupted by telemarketers at dinner. Now, with concerns over Internet privacy rising all the time, the same types of options may be coming online soon, in the form of a "do not track" online option.

Although there's still some debate about how – and whether – this kind of technology could really work, it will be interesting to see what the general public thinks about it. After all, online tracking sounds a little bit creepy, but it does have some benefits, such as better, more targeted advertising, faster logins to the sites you use, etc.

So, what are the implications of a debate on "do not track?" Here are a few quick things to keep in mind:

Laws about every part of the Internet are changing.

As we saw with SOPA, the Internet represents the old Wild West in a lot of ways. Not only are the laws always changing, but they're having a hard time keeping up with the growth in different areas and ideas that keep popping up. What is legal and illegal to tweet? How do copyrights apply to image-sharing sites? How much privacy are users entitled to when looking through different websites?

There aren't clear answers to these questions, and the legislation around them is bound to keep shifting.

No matter what, it's up to you to protect your privacy.

While the laws might change, the risks from the wrong types of people probably won't. As a simple analogy, consider that laws against things like burglary, mugging, etc., don't completely eliminate these problems, regardless of the penalties. As long as there is money to be made from stealing over the Internet – and all indications are that those sums are growing, not shrinking – there are going to be thieves online.

For that reason, it's up to individual users to take the necessary steps to protect themselves (like using a firewall and updating your antivirus software frequently) as a first line of defense.

Most of what people find out about you isn't from some scary database.

Although it's convenient to fear "master hackers" hidden within shady bunkers in third-world countries, the reality is that most online thefts aren't the product of criminal super-geniuses... they are from the equivalent of leaving our front doors open and unlocked. That's because lots of us don't think twice about what we share on our blogs, social media profiles, e-mails, and other communications.

If you want better online security – and want to reduce the odds of becoming a victim of identity theft and other forms of fraud – it's important not to make yourself an easy target. Use your head and don't share anything you want to keep from the world over the Internet.

A "do not track" list may or may not be coming in the near future, but Internet security is going to continue to be a big topic either way. Are you as safe with your browsing and posting as you should be?

TECHNOLOGY AT YOUR FINGERTIPS

I recently attended a comedy show and the comedian asked that people put their phones away and appreciate the "experience". I laughed but realized that many people are missing out on what's happening around them. I saw a video on Facebook of one of my friends on stage with one of my favorite bands. I thought, "You are on stage with 30 Seconds to Mars – on your phone?" How can you appreciate an experience like that when you are worried if your phone is picking it up. Sure, you may want to document it for proof to show your friends but now you missed out on the experience.

There are dozens of YouTube videos of people falling or running into things because they are so caught up in texting while walking and not watching where they are going. Or worse yet, texting while driving – apparently we need to tell people that it isn't safe. People are so worried about staying connected that they risk their lives.

Maybe I feel this way because I grew up in a non-technology era. I remember my friend telling me the Beatles wrote the song "Hey Jude" about his sister, Judy, who was friends with the band. Even though I knew he was lying, we couldn't just Google it to prove he was making it up. In fact, there really wasn't any way of finding out if his story was true. Even the local library would have a hard time providing proof. But now, a quick Google search tells me the song was written for John Lennon's son. I'm not even a Beatles fan, but the point I'm trying to make is that fact finding missions are almost too easy now.

Don't get me wrong. I love technology!

I make a living on my computer and love learning something new every day. But I think we should all ignore technology once in a while. Even when it's working really well, technology is no substitute for friends, family, and the other things we love. It doesn't matter if you make your living with computers (as I do), make a point of getting away from them once in a while. You'll find that you'll appreciate them a lot more when you come back, not to mention having a few memories not documented on your phone!

EMAIL – FAST CONVERSATIONS AND MANNERS

This morning I woke up to a scorching email from someone. This is a professional woman who I do not know. I bet it took a good hour to type this email out. It rambled on and on the first paragraph then just got mean towards the end. At first, I thought it was a junk mail but soon realized she was angry when she was typing. I was shocked that someone in her position would write something like this to someone she didn't know or anyone for that matter.

Later this morning, I got another email from her which I considered deleting before reading it. It was an apology for her rant from the night before. Something I learned long ago is waiting before sending emails, which is what I did with my response. In Outlook, you can save your rant email as a draft until morning, re-read it, then hit send. I recommend this.

Email is great for fast conversations, asking a quick question or having a message waiting for someone. It is NOT great for venting. I thought I would use this email opportunity to give a few tips for sending a professional email.

1. **Always use a salutation.** "Dear You," or "Hello Name" – this way the person knows the email is to them.

2. **Don't write when you are angry.** If you want answers, pick up the phone.

3. **DON'T TYPE IN CAPITAL LETTERS.** This is considered yelling in electronic correspondence.

4. **This is a pet peeve of mine:** Don't use excessive punctuation!!! Ask your question with on question mark. Maybe it's just me, but does multiple question marks look annoying????

5. **Always thank someone and sign your name to an email.** Have some type of closing such as "Thanks for your time, Tammy" Then sign your name.

I think we will all agree in this day and age of fast correspondence and texting, people have sometimes forgotten their manners. I hope these tips can help someone from an embarrassing situation of trying to un-send an email they wished they hadn't sent.

BECOME AN INTERNET KNOW-IT-ALL

"The only things worth learning are the things you learn after you know it all." – Harry Truman

When it comes to the internet, no one knows it all. If a person does actually know something about computers, it can change the next day with a simple upgrade. When working with computers and the internet, you can potentially learn something new every day! I love Jimmy Fallon's character, Nick Burns the computer guy on Saturday Night Live, who is annoyed because his co-workers ask him a computer question. He makes them move away from their desks, as his fingers fly around on the keyboard and he shows off with his condescending "tech talk". Thank goodness, not all people in the computer support industry are like this.

Asking questions will get you answers. Do not be afraid to try to figure things out for yourself. The internet is probably the most giving place on earth. Most people are willing to share their knowledge and ideas through their websites. This is what keeps visitors coming back!

Google it! Google.com

There are thousands of support sites or message boards out there. I thought I would share some of my favorite computer support links. It was hard to narrow down my favorites, but here are a few websites that have answers to almost everything.

Mashable mashable.com

If a person had a question about social media such as Twitter or Facebook, the answer would be on this website. In fact, just about any tech question can be answered here. It is a great resource for anyone interested in where technology is going. Join the mailing list and get the top articles of the day in your inbox.

CNet cnet.com

Years ago, this was the website a person visited when they wanted to download a program. Cnet ran a popular site called download.com which has now integrated into Cnet. This website does not care if you are a MAC or PC because all information is popular.

Tech Crunch techcrunch.com

From start-ups to gadgets, this is the site to check for new gadgets, like the Solar Kindle cover and Android apps. As a news junkie, I appreciate the depth of this website.

Often, computers and the internet can be intimidating. Security, data, crashes and hackers, it is sometimes a scary place. But arming yourself with a bit of knowledge will make all the difference in the world.

HOW 60 SECONDS ONLINE CAN MAKE YOUR WHOLE DAY

I spend a lot of time in my business, thinking about the practical, nuts-and-bolts aspects of the Internet: How do we use it better, what can it do for your research, business or career, etc.?

It's a fun field, because there are always lots of fascinating answers to these questions. Every once in a while, though, I like to take a step back and get a little more philosophical about things and ask questions like, "What is the Internet really for?"

I've decided that the answer is a bit like the meaning of life – it probably depends on who you are and what you want it to be. One thing that it should be, however, is a tool for making your life a bit better and more enjoyable.

I bring this up because the novelty of the Internet wore off for a lot of us many years ago. It's no longer as much "fun" to go online when we are thinking about work, research, and responsibilities. That's understandable, but it's also a bit of a waste; there's a lot of really fun stuff you can find out there in cyberspace, and you don't have to waste a big chunk of your day getting to it.

In fact, to help readers get more from the time they're spending online, here are a few things I've noticed that can make your whole day. Best of all, most of them can be finished in a minute or less:

Tell or learn a joke.

Nothing beats humor in the middle of a tough workday, and sharing one of your own jokes, or learning one that someone else has posted, is a great way to brighten the world around you. JokesPlace.com will give you a good start.

Pick up a new recipe.

It's easy to fall into a rut in the kitchen, and there are literally millions of great recipes out there on easy-to-find websites. Why not spice up your week, literally, with something new? Recipe.com is a great place to get started – and yes, they are free.

Make a donation or micro-loan.

One of the oldest pieces of advice in the world is still one of the most powerful: The best way to make yourself feel better and pick up your mood is by doing something great for someone else. You'd be amazed at what one random act of kindness can do for your daily outlook. Kiva. org is a non-profit who can change lives with just a $25 loan.

Do a favor for a stranger.

There are a lot of ways to be charitable, even if you aren't working with an organized charitable group. There are lots of forms online where you can do things like answer questions for students, contribute creatively to a collaborative project, or otherwise help out someone else. Look local – there are many organizations that have probably helped someone you know.

Write a positive review.

It's sad, but many of us only take the time to share our thoughts and impressions when we're angry. It's just as easy (and a lot less stressful) to pass along a good word now and then. Google them and then write a review or use sites like Urban Spoon or Trip Advisor for eateries.

As I mentioned, none of these has to take much of your time, but whatever piece of your calendar you do give is bound to come back to you several times over in the form of a better mood. There's a lot to be said for making the most of the Internet as a business or research tool, but why shouldn't you take a few moments to brighten up your day online?

THE EASIEST WAY TO START A PROFITABLE COMPANY ONLINE

Earlier, I showed how you could create your next online job over the Internet, helping you to make a few hundred extra dollars – or more – each and every week. Today, I want to share the secrets of starting an Internet company that's profitable right away: Find a very tightly defined niche and market directly to it.

The Internet has made it possible to reach small groups of buyers more cost-effectively than ever. That's important, because instead of trying to compete with the Wal-Marts, Best Buys, and Staples of the world, the easiest way to carve out a market isn't to think bigger, but smaller. In other words, instead of trying to find millions of customers, you should be searching for a small, committed few who will buy from you again and again.

As an example, let's say you are part of a small community that revolves around a certain interest or hobby (like rock climbers in southern Illinois). There might not be a lot of people in that group, but they will be easy to find, and more importantly, cost-effective to reach through online ads, specialty websites, and even local newsletters.

By coming up with a blog, website, or online store devoted just to them, you can carve out an instant market niche that would be hard for others to break into. To stay with our rock-climbing example, you could set up a website with travel advice, home training guides, and specialized products. The profits might not be enormous, but you aren't going to have many competitors, either, and it won't be hard to build a business that's consistently profitable.

Not into scaling icy peaks? That's no problem, it was just a quick example, and the possibilities are virtually endless. No matter what your idea or passion is, it's the niche that helps you find profits. Here are a few tips to help you get started with your own targeted online venture:

Choose a domain name that's easy to remember and understand.

Your website's URL is essentially your address in the virtual world. Make sure to choose one that's easy to find and remember, because it's a decision that can literally make or break your new online business.

Start with a simple website.

You don't have to go overboard with your design (or budget) for your new online business. Instead of trying to be the biggest and best, simply focus on being the easiest for your customers to use. You can always grow from there.

Always focus on your customer, not your company.

Speaking of your customers, think of everything in your online store from their point of view. What sort of content and products would they want to find in your site? The better you can answer that question, the more successful you are likely to be.

Examine the competition for positives and negatives.

Even if you don't have any direct competitors for your niche market, take a look at related sites to see what they are doing well, as well as which areas you think you could improve upon.

Develop a consistent marketing strategy.

If there were one mistake I could point to that ruins a lot of online businesses, it would be seeing marketing as a one-time activity. Develop a mindset of continual effort, and you'll build a business that attracts new customers reliably and consistently.

Experiment over time to grow your business.

Success can be as dangerous as failure, if you let it stop you from trying new things. Always stick with what's working, but don't be afraid to branch out and explore new opportunities, either.

THE (SECOND) GREATEST THING ABOUT MAKING MONEY ONLINE

Last week I devoted time talking about different ways that people could start making a bit of money online specifically by doing things like opening an online store or trying their hand at freelance projects. Biased as I might be, I think that generating money over the Internet is one of the greatest things that can happen to you, if only because it can give you a new sense of freedom in a shaky and uncertain economy. Plus, it's easy to get started and lots of fun once you do.

One of the things that I might not have emphasized enough, however, is that making money online doesn't have to be an "all or nothing" kind of proposition; you can give it a try in your spare time while holding down your 9-to-5 job. That's important, because one of the greatest things about an Internet business is that it can help you reach the dreams you already have faster.

What could you save for with an Internet business? How about things like:

A new car.

Although this is a common dream, it could just as easily be an addition to your home, or virtually any other big-ticket purchase. Instead of looking into financing, or putting it off for another few years, why not get your online store or other online business humming along to the point where you can easily make the payments from the revenue you saved?

A dream vacation.

In the same way, even a few hundred dollars a month can put that trip to Bora Bora within reach. If you've been longing for an extended getaway, that could be just the motivation you need to get your new business moving. And best of all? After you earn your dream vacation, you can just start saving for the next one!

A college education.

For many students and their parents, the choice to go to a great school is a bittersweet one, since it can mean relying heavily on student loans or cutting back on the things they've gotten used to enjoying in the past. Over the period of a few years, however, an even moderately successful Internet business can cover the cost of a good education, and maybe a few books and pizzas as well.

Your retirement.

It's no secret that more and more of us are working later in life, both to stay active and to enjoy a higher standard of living. Not only can an online business open the door to those possibilities, but also let you choose to work with the field or topic you really enjoy. For those who are looking ahead to the golden years, or want to try semi-retirement, an online business can be the perfect answer.

I bring up these possibilities for two reasons. First, because having short- and long-term goals can help you create the motivation and urgency that it takes to stop watching others succeed and get out there to make your own success. And secondly, because each of these is absolutely realistic – although few people become "Internet millionaires" overnight anymore, there are tens of thousands of people just like you, from all ages and backgrounds, using the Internet to supplement the cash flow they get from their regular jobs.

It costs you virtually nothing but a little bit of dreaming to explore these opportunities, so my question to you is: What are you waiting for? What dream could you be moving closer to today?

In closing

I hope these articles were helpful to you. I really want you to succeed in whatever you do. Set your goals and stick with them, even when someone tells you no. You can do it!